The Black

Know what you believe and why!

Foundational Theology
Truth Every Christian Should Know

Christian Karate Association

1

Christian Karate Association
christiankarate.org

Black Belt Christian
© 2022 by 1Karate LLC.

979-8-3622-1582-8

The Christian Karate
Association brand and logo
used by permission.
Copyright © 2022 by the
Christian Karate Association.

Unless otherwise noted,
Scripture quotations are taken
from the Holy Bible, English
Standard Version. All rights
reserved.

Author:
Steven A. Wilson Sr.
Chief Chaplain – CKA

Published in the USA

Table of Contents

Foundational Theology
Truth Every Christian Should Know

By Steven A. Wilson, PhD

Even though most Christians have been in the church for a long time, many lack even a general understanding of important Christian beliefs and principles. The purpose of this study is not to provide an exhaustive analysis of any subject but rather it is designed to give a general overview of some important topics and encourage further study.

Scripture quotations are taken from the English Standard Version Translation. In most cases I have written out the entire verse since I have discovered that Scriptural references are often overlooked or ignored. The biblical references are more important than the commentary or discussion since they are where the truth is discovered.

Serious Bible students should familiarize themselves with the original Hebrew and Greek or consider multiple translations. Good translations in addition to the English Standard Translation include the New International Version and the New American Standard Bible. It is very important for you to get into the habit of looking up all of the Scriptural references quoted in these studies in your own Bible. Most individuals, including Christians, are biblically illiterate and have difficulty finding the references in their own Bible. The only way to really know and understand God's Word is to read, study and memorize it. I encourage you to mark up your Bible as you go. Highlight verses that personally speak to you. Make notes in the margins and write your reactions to the verses. I have personally done that with several different versions of the entire Bible. A Bible that you work through will make a great gift to your children or grandchildren. Wouldn't you like to have a Bible your grandparent studied and wrote in?

A tool that is helpful in discipleship is to take notes on your study. Some people keep a notebook or a journal to record their insights, questions, ideas and even prayers.

Much of the approach to this study will be done as though I am speaking directly to you on a personal basis. I will also include some illustrations from my own experiences as well as anecdotes and stories that highlight or enhance the topic at hand. An important point that you should keep in mind is that this is written from my own perspective. I have been a Christian for many years as well as a pastor, chaplain and Bible teacher. My formal education has been in liberal arts, religion, psychology, philosophy and theology. I have read and studied the entire Bible many times. My experiences have also included extensive interaction with various religious and non-religious groups and ideas.

As you work through this study remember that the Bible is the final authority on what is true and what is not. If what you have been taught or what you believe is different from what I am going to tell you then consider my arguments in the light of Scripture and make changes to your theology and worldview if necessary.

Section 1
Introduction

1. How do you measure up?

According to the Bible, Christian maturity is not an option but a necessity. Occasionally I have a reoccurring dream in which I am in college and the quarter is coming to an end when I discover that I have registered for a class but never attended it. Panic and frustration ensue as I try, in my dream, to decide if I should drop the class or just take a failing grade. Christians should be life-long learners. Personally I can't understand why someone would neglect such a wonderful experience of learning more about the God who loves us enough to create us, redeem us and give us eternal life. How does the following verse speak to you?

"About this we have much to say, and it is hard to explain, since you have become dull of hearing. For though by this time you ought to be teachers, you need someone to teach you again the basic principles of the oracles of God. You need milk, not solid food, for everyone who lives on milk is unskilled in the word of righteousness, since he is a child. But solid food is for the mature, for those who have their powers of discernment trained by constant practice to distinguish good from evil." (Hebrews 5:11-14)

2. The Importance of Determination

When I was 36 years old I attended the U.S. Army Airborne School. I was considered an "old man" in the program since most of the soldiers were much younger. Needless to say the physical and psychological stress was tremendous! Even though it was very difficult, I was determined to be successful. One day a young soldier told me that he was watching me and he knew that if I could make it then he could as well. I didn't know whether to take that as an insult or a compliment! I do know that I felt a great sense of accomplishment when, at the end of the training, they pinned the coveted airborne wings on my chest.

Spiritual growth, maturity and understanding can be a difficult challenge. Some theological and philosophic concepts can seem strange and incomprehensible at first but don't give up. With hard work and the insight given by the Holy Spirit you can develop a firm foundation for further exciting exploration into the wonders of God. There may have been a time in your life when you were really excited about learning about God but you have since lost your zeal. Now is a good time to forget about your past failures and discouragements and start fresh! God wants you to move ahead and discover a deeper and richer Christian experience!
Regarding his own spiritual development the Apostle Paul wrote: "Not that I have already obtained this or am already perfect, but I press on to make it my own, because Christ Jesus has made me his own. Brothers, I do not consider that I have made it my own. But one thing I do: forgetting what lies behind and straining forward to what lies ahead, I press on toward the goal for the prize of the upward call of God in Christ Jesus." Philippians 3:12-14

3. Why Study Theology?

Why study theology? That's a good question. Why not study something fun like comic books or video game strategies? The study of theology might sound boring. Yet, studying about certain things in life might just be worth the effort. For example studying a book on how to wire your house might be better than blowing your socks off by touching the wrong wire! Just what is so important about understanding theology? Understanding theology is crucial because what comes into our minds when we think about God is the most important thing about us! Our belief or non-belief in God and what He is like influences everything we do and determines our eternal destiny. It is vital, therefore, for us to have as accurate an understanding of God as is possible.

Simply stated, the word theology is made up of two Greek words: theos = God and logos = a discourse (word) thus theology is a discourse or the study of God.

4. What is Important and What is Not

Important Word
Doctrine: "A particular principle, position, or policy taught or advocated, as of a religion or government."

It has been said that you should never discuss religion or politics. Wars have even been fought over what later was determined to be insignificant issues. The reason for many of the conflicts is because those subjects can often result in very emotional arguments. Often without any logical understanding. In studying theology it is important to distinguish between foundational, essential and non-essential doctrines. A foundational doctrine is one that is clearly taught in Scripture and is universally understood by all mature Christians as being true. An example would be a belief in the Trinity or the Divinity of Christ since that directly relates to who God really is. On those doctrines we must remain dogmatic and allow for no compromise

An essential doctrine would be one that is required for salvation. Simply stated it would include an acknowledgement of sin and a repentance (turning away) from sin, a willingness to follow the Bible and its teachings to the best of the person's understanding and a belief and acceptance of the atoning work of Christ on the cross. A non-essential doctrine is usually one that is open to many interpretations such as the specific details regarding the return of Christ and the end of the world. Tolerance for a difference of opinion in non-essential doctrines is encouraged and should be respected.

5. Types of Theology

The study of theology is vast and it is impossible to understand everything there is to know about God. Anyone who has ever seriously studied any subject in detail knows that often the more you study the more you realize that there is a lot that you don't know! But every bit of information we discover can help us to experience the abundant life God wants for us. Remember Jesus said in _John 10:10 "I came that they may have life and have it abundantly."_ Because of what Jesus accomplished on the cross we now have access to God in a much more intimate way. Years of study about God will enrich your understanding of Him and will lead you to exciting discoveries that will fill your life with joy and blessing.

Any discussion, writing or study of God could be considered theology, but in regard to the Christian faith, the study of theology could be understood as falling under one of the following categories:

1. Systematic Theology – Systematically state the contents of the Christian Faith.

2. Historical Theology – The history of Christian thought.

3. Moral Theology – Christian living – Ethics

4. Applied Theology – Pastoral Ministry – Missions – Christian Education

The focus of this study will be primarily, but not exclusively, on Systematic Theology. As stated before, this is not an exhaustive study but rather an overview of doctrines essential to Christian understanding. While not everyone will agree with my conclusions, I would encourage you to carefully study the doctrines for yourself with a willingness to embrace or change your views if convinced by the Holy Spirit and Scripture. Several times I have discussed doctrine with people clearly pointing out Scriptures to support my position only to be rejected with the argument, "We've always believed and been taught differently." Continuing to believe a false doctrine in spite of the evidence is not only foolish but can also be dangerous.

6. How we Develop our Understanding of Theology

It is amazing to discover the different ways that people develop their understanding of God. Usually it happens according to our parent's views, our upbringing, or the environment we find ourselves in. Few people really take the time to sincerely search, study and analyze their thinking about God. As a matter of fact most people who attend church really don't know what their specific church believes as important teachings. This is especially true with the movement away from denominations that have well known established doctrines and policies to so-called "non-denominational" churches. That is really tragic when you think about it. The most important thing in the world is given so little attention! I have known of people who have attended churches based on the entertainment value or popularity that clearly teach unbiblical doctrines and ideas! Some groups place great importance in being "seeker friendly" and refuse to preach or teach biblical values that might offend the person attending. This is especially evident in the avoidance of teaching Biblical morality specifically in regard to sexual conduct. How about you? Do you know the specific doctrines of the church or Bible study group you attend? Do you know the theology of your friends and family? Is your own moral conduct in line with the demands of Scripture? Do you know what those demands are?

A note about denominations: any church or group of churches, large or small is really a "denomination" in itself. A denomination is just a group of religious people, churches or fellowships or individuals that all believe essentially the same thing. So, in reality, there is no such thing as a "non-denominational" church.

7. Wesley's Quadrilateral

Now back to our discussion. Many years ago a deeply devout Christian, who was the founder of the Methodist movement, by the name of John Wesley, suggested that doctrinal truth should be understood and established by following certain steps. This is known in theology as Wesley's Quadrilateral. What he taught was not a new idea but he made it more concise and easier to understand.

Wesley said that there are four steps to determining Biblical truth. The four steps are listed in order of importance. Scripture is supreme. None of the points following Scripture can contradict the clear teachings of the Bible.

1. Scripture – What are the clearly stated truths of Scripture?

2. History – What has the Church believed on this subject?

3. Logic – Does the idea make sense?

4. Experience – What is my personal experience regarding the issue?

Too many people get the order all messed up. Often people base their beliefs on what "feels good to me" or "what makes sense to me" rather than on what the Scriptures teach. This is especially true with the passages that talk of the wrath of God or God's Judgment. I mean, who wants a God that is mad at them? Others simply believe what is popular at the moment. Religious fads can sweep through the church and create much confusion and sometimes even causes great harm to the Kingdom of God.

But really, when you get right down to it, being right is more important than being wrong and feeling good about it! Sincerity in believing the wrong thing can be disastrous! When I was a kid growing up on the ranch we used to use old gallon jugs to put our drinking water in. One day my little brother tipped back a jug and began to drink only to discover that it was bleach! Truth is more important that sincerity.

Important Word
Heresy: opinion or doctrine at variance with the orthodox or accepted doctrine, especially of a church or religious system.

Church History Moment
The history of the Christian Church has been plagued with heretical ideas that have challenged the understanding of God and His nature. If satan can't get you to stop believing in God then he will try to get you to believe lies about God and His plan for you.

One of the most powerful influences in the early Church was the rise of a group known as Gnosticism. The primary view was that spiritual things were good and material things were bad. Therefore Jesus could not be God in the flesh. In practical lifestyle, some Gnostics thought that since your body is evil you can let it do whatever it wants. Kind of the old 60's motto: "If it feels good do it!" Others said that if the body is evil then you shouldn't do anything that brought physical pleasure (obviously this group soon died out).

Section 2
The Nature of God

I've got news for you. You're not God. Surprised? God is an infinite being. His creation is finite. No matter how important you think you are, you are still way short of being God! Of course, that's not the way a lot of people act. Most people are basically self-centered and expect the world to revolve around them. When a famous, arrogant movie star was talking with a friend she said, "I'm tired of talking about myself. Let's talk about you. How did you like my last movie?"

When we begin to understand the nature of God we begin to see that there is a big difference between Him and us. It's like we are riding around on our rusty tricycle thinking we are really cool and God shows up in his brand new sports car. Actually the difference is greater than that. By far!

It is impossible for us to fully describe the nature of The Almighty. Our puny brains simply cannot grasp the fullness of God. All of our understanding of God is to some degree limited. The Bible makes it very clear that *"For now we see in a mirror dimly, but then face to face. Now I know in part; then I shall know fully, even as I have been fully known." (1 Corinthians 13:12)*

Important Word
Theological Anthropomorphism
If you are going to study theology you are going to run into some big words. One of my favorites is anthropomorphism. Not only is it impressive to quote to your friends but it also really helps us figure

out why we can't totally comprehend God. The Bible says that _"God is spirit, and those who worship him must worship in spirit and truth." (John 4:24)_ Part of our problem with gaining a proper perspective of God is that we are attempting to describe God, who is infinite, in human, finite, terms. This especially relates to ascribing to God human characteristics.

The Old Testament often uses descriptive language in referring to God or His nature. It describes God as "walking," "being angry," "smelling," "repenting"; refers to His "arms," "feet," "eyes," "ears," "hands"; says He is like a woman screaming in childbirth _(Isaiah 42:14)_, a beast tearing it's prey _(Hosea 13:8)_ and a moth eating a garment _(Hosea 5:12)_. Wow! That really conjures up some strange images.

In the New Testament God is generally not described in such vivid anthropomorphic terms. However, the incarnation, the ultimate anthropomorphism, speaks of both God's immanence (God being in, but apart, from the material world) and His livingness (God is a living being). What that means in plain English is that the nature of Jesus is the revelation of what God is like. This includes the whole description of Him. We love the Gospels, which speak a lot about God's love and forgiveness but don't overlook the Book of Revelation! The Gospels present Jesus as the Savior of lost mankind. The Book of Revelation shows Jesus as the Judge of the ungodly. When Jesus came to earth He demonstrated the exact nature of God. _"In Christ lives all the fullness of God in a human body." (Colossians 2:9)_

Any way you look at it, it is hard to describe the indescribable. So don't get uptight if there are some things about God you can't understand. There is enough we do know, if we look for it, to get and keep us on the right track. _"For his invisible attributes, namely, his eternal power and divine nature, have been clearly perceived, ever since the creation of the world, in the things that have been made. So they are without excuse." (Romans 1:20)_

1. Definition of God
The Bible does not contain a definition of God. How could it? The nearest approach to anything like a definition is found in the words

of Jesus to the Samaritan woman, *"God is Spirit" (John 4:24)*. Since God is a Spirit He has none of the properties belonging to matter, and as a result He cannot be discerned by the bodily senses unless he takes a material form or appears to take that form. Sometimes the Old Testament calls pre-incarnate appearances of Jesus "The Angel of the Lord." At other times the angel of the Lord is just a messenger of God. The context of the verses help you to understand which is which *(See Genesis 16)*.

Important Word
Theophany: The appearance of God in a way that is perceived by humans. Theophanies of the Old Testament include appearances to: Adam *(Genesis 3:8)*, Abraham *(Genesis17:1-4, 9-10, 15-16, 22; Genesis 18:1-3,10)*, Jacob *(Genesis 32:24-30)*, Moses *(Exodus 3:2-6)*, Joshua *(Joshua 5:13-15)*, and Daniel *(Daniel 3:22-25)*.

Just try to describe someone without using physical attributes. It's kind of like when you're in high school and someone suggests that you go out with someone on a blind date. You ask what they are like and they say something like, "She has a good personality." That is certainly something you would want in a date but it also often meant that they weren't much to look at. (It is interesting to note that there is no physical description of Jesus. God obviously knows that indeed, personal character is more important than what we look like on the outside.)

Even though it is impossible to completely define God, we can however describe certain characteristics of God as illustrated in Scripture.

2. The Absolute Attributes of God
Whenever we consider the attributes of God the first thing that we need to understand is that we cannot understand. Say what? Remember that since God is infinite then our feeble attempts at understanding His attributes will always be limited. As a matter of fact, I believe that there are attributes of God that we will not know until we are in heaven with Him. There are clear teachings in Scripture, however, that can reveal to us some amazing things about God.

For the sake of discussion we will divide the attributes of God into two major categories: 1) The Absolute Attributes of God and 2) The Moral Attributes of God. The absolute attributes of God are characteristics that only belong to Him. You don't have them, satan doesn't have them and your favorite super hero doesn't have them. The Moral Attributes are aspects that each person should have since we have been made in the image of God but may have been damaged, distorted or destroyed due to sin. Let's first take a look at the Absolute Attributes of God.

Sovereignty

The first attribute for us to consider is the sovereignty of God. This is an attribute that is confusing to many. Does God make everything happen? Even evil? To say that God is responsible for evil is to deny his justice and holiness. Sovereignty as it relates to God in its simplest understanding is to realize that God can do whatever He wants. He is not externally limited in any way. The only limitation is that He does not contradict His nature. For example, God cannot lie: *"So when God desired to show more convincingly to the heirs of the promise the unchangeable character of his purpose, he guaranteed it with an oath, so that by two unchangeable things, in which it is impossible for God to lie, we who have fled for refuge might have strong encouragement to hold fast to the hope set before us." (Hebrews 6:17-18)*

He sets the rules and governs all creation as He wants. His will for everything can be divided into two areas: 1) His determined will and 2) His allowed will. His determined will is that there are certain things that he makes happen. Biblical prophecies are an example. This would also include the normal natural laws of the universe. If you jump off the roof you will hit the ground because God has established the law of gravity that will always happen unless He intervenes. His allowed will can be understood as the areas where God allows a person, or creature, different choices from which to choose. For humans this can be understood as free will. God never takes away a person's free will. Our purpose and happiness in life and our eternal destiny are always dependent on the choices we make.

Unity

God's unity was perhaps emphasized more than any other of God's attributes in the Old Testament and is re-emphasized in the New Testament. God is one. He is unique unto himself. *(Deuteronomy 4:35; 6:4; 32:39; I Samuel 7:22; II Kings 19:15; Isaiah 44:6, 8; 45:5; John 17:3; I Corinthians 8:4, 6; Ephesians 4:6; I Timothy 1:17; James 2:19)* The teachings of the Bible regarding the fact that there is only one God is unique. Polytheism, the view that there are many gods, was predominate in the thinking of the majority of people throughout history.

The idea of monotheism (only one God) is a fundamental doctrine of Christians, Jews and Muslims. For the Jews every day they include this principle in their prayers. This is known as the Shema. It is a quote from *Deuteronomy 6:4 "Hear, O Israel: The Lord our God, the Lord is one."*

Infinite

The term infinite refers to that perfection of God by which He is free from all limitations. God can do anything that he wants. And, unlike us, whatever God wants to do is always good and holy. He is also not limited by the created world (time-space relationships).
There's an old discussion going around that asks, "Can God make a rock bigger than He can lift?" Either way you answer the question you are suggesting that there are some things that God cannot do. I like the answer my wife gave. She said, "Yes, God can make a rock bigger than he can lift and then he could lift it." The only limitations of God are self-imposed or inherent in His nature. God cannot lie, sin, change, or deny himself. *(Numbers 23:19; 1 Samuel 15:29; 2 Timothy 2:13; Hebrews 6:18; James 1:13, 17)*

Self-Existence

God has no origin. He is uncreated and depends on nothing. All things in our material world had to begin at some time. Aside from God, nothing is self-caused. The mere existence of things indicates that there must be someone or something that caused the things to come into existence. I was never very good in math but one thing I do know is that nothing plus nothing still equals nothing. If I don't have any money and I give it all to you and you don't have any money and you give it all to me we are both still broke!

A fundamental law in science is the law of cause and affect. Simply put, the law of cause and effect states that every material effect must have an adequate cause that existed before the effect. If one goes back far enough one has to accept a self-existent being that is able to create. Only a believer in God can answer the question, "What was before that?" *(Exodus 3:14; John 5:26; Psalm 94:8ff, Isaiah 40:18ff; Acts 17:25; Romans 11:33-34; Ephesians 1:5; Revelation 4:11)*

Eternality
"You're traveling through another dimension, a dimension not only of sight and sound but of mind. A journey into a wondrous land whose boundaries are that of imagination. That's the signpost up ahead - your next stop, the Twilight Zone!" So goes the quote from the popular television series in the early 1960's. I was always fascinated by the show. To think that there were dimensions that were beyond normal experiences was intriguing. And even though the show was fiction it really had an element of truth in it. There is another realm that is not physical or controlled by time. That is eternity. Time and space, including all matter, was created by God. That is the dimension we currently live in.

God is eternal. He is timeless. He exists outside the categories of time or space as well as within time and space. *(Genesis 21:33; Psalm 90:2; Isaiah 57:15; 1 Timothy 1:17 Deuteronomy 33:27; 93:2; 103:24, 27; Isaiah 94:6; 57:15; Hebrews 1:12; I Timothy 1:17; Revelation 1:4, 8.)*

Immutability
We had a poster in our church nursery that said: *"Behold, I tell you a mystery; we will not all sleep, but we will all be changed" (1 Corinthians 15:51)*. Sounds appropriate for a nursery!

It has been said that one of the constants of life is that everything changes. An ancient philosopher by the name of Heraclitus once said that you can never step in the same stream twice because no matter how fast you are, the stream is different when you step back in. That may be true about our physical world but it is not true about

17

God. God is unchanging in his nature. A perfect being cannot increase or decrease in any respect. God does not change in regard to His being, in relation to His promises, or in respect to His works. God, as absolute perfection, neither improvement nor deterioration is possible. Malachi states it precisely: *"I the Lord do not change." (Malachi 3:6). (See also: Exodus 3:14; Psalm 102:26-28; Isaiah 41:4; Hebrews 1:11-12; 6:17; James 1:17; John 8:58; Numbers 23:19; 1 Samuel 15:29; Job 23:13; Psalm 102:27; Isaiah 26:4.)* The fact that God does not change brings comfort to those who trust in Him but should cause fear in those who hope God will change his mind about punishing the wicked. *(Psalm 1:21-22; Romans 2:2-11; 4:20-21; I Thessalonians 5:24)*

Omnipresence

A frustrated person once said, "Everywhere I go I go too and that ruins everything!" No matter what we do we can't escape ourselves. The same can be said about God. He is present everywhere in creation. Though God remains distinct from creation and may not be identified with the world, yet He is present in every part of His creation. The omnipresence of God is a basic teaching of the Bible. This is both good news and bad news. It is a comfort to know that He is always available but can also be a bit unsettling to know that He sees everything we do! *(1 Kings 8:27; Isaiah 66:1; Acts 7:48-49; Psalm 139:7-10; Jeremiah 23:23-24; Acts 17:27-28; Ephesians 1:23)*

Omniscience

Ever know someone that seemed to know everything? I knew a man like that once. I asked him how he knew so much. He told me that when he was a boy in school one of his teachers made fun of him because he didn't know the answer to a question so he went home and read through a whole set of encyclopedias! I would have forgotten most of what I read but he had a very good memory.

God knows all that is knowable. His knowledge is inclusive and comprehensive. He knows himself and all that comes from Him. He knows all things, past, present, and future. He knows all relations and relationships. He knows what is actual and what is possible. The omniscience of God is a distinct revelation in Scripture. God's knowledge is perfect. *(Job 37:16)*; He knows the inner heart of each person *(1 Samuel 16:7; 1 Chronicles 28:9; Psalm 139:14; Jeremiah 17:10)*. God sees the behavior of all people *(Deuteronomy 2:7; Job 23:10; 24:23; Psalm 1:6; Psalm 37:18)*. God also knows about future events *(1 Samuel 23:10-12; 2 Kings 13:19; Psalm 81:14-15; Isaiah 42:9; Ezekiel 3:6; Matthew 11:21; the whole book of Revelation)*.

It is important to understand that even though God knows everything that will happen He doesn't cause everything to happen. If that were the case then he would be responsible for evil and indiscriminate pain in the world, which is impossible for God. Knowing something will happen and making it happen are two different things.

Omnipotence
In the 1970s there was a popular television program entitled The Six Million Dollar Man. It was about an astronaut who crashes and is rebuilt by the government using bionics. He was now part man and part machine. His incredible strength and speed (up to 60 mph) made him a super hero. It made for an entertaining program but really, in spite of man's attempts to become all-powerful, we will never even begin to compare with God.

God has perfect and complete power. By the exercise of His will, God can realize whatever is present in His will. The Bible is emphatic in speaking of the Lord God Almighty *(Job 9:12; Psalm 115:3; Jeremiah 32:17; Matthew 19:26; Luke 1:37; Romans 1:20; Ephesians 1:19)*; God reveals His power in creation *(Isaiah 44:24; Romans 4:17)*; in works of providence *(Hebrews 1:3)*, and in the redemption of sinners (Yes, that means you!). *(Romans 1:16; 1 Corinthians 1:24)* (See also: *Genesis 17:1; Isaiah 26:4; 43:13; Jeremiah 27:5; Daniel 4:35; Revelation 1:8; 19:6.)*

3. The Moral Attributes of God
The moral attributes of God are those things about God that he is able, to some degree, to impart to human beings.

Wisdom
One of the things that is common among us is the ability to make bad decisions. Every person alive has regrets about what he or she has done in the past. A sign of maturity is to learn from our

mistakes but it seems like most people never do. As a matter of fact many people make a lifestyle of poor choices. It would be good to realize that two stupids don't make a smart! One of the truths of history is that history repeats itself, often with terrible consequences.

There is only One who never makes a bad decision. The wisdom of God is evident from the works of creation, providence, and redemption, and from express declarations of Scripture. *(Exodus 34:6; Ps. 54:24; Proverbs 3:19; 8:14; Jeremiah 10:12; Daniel 2:20; Romans 11:33; 1 Corinthians 3:19; Colossians 2:3; Jude 25; Revelation 5:12)*

Holiness

Holiness in the Old Testament basically means separation and purity. *(Exodus 29:43; Leviticus 10:3; 11:44; Joshua 24:19; Psalm 22:3; 111:9; 145:17; Isaiah 6:3; 10:17; 1 Kings 8:10-11; Exodus 13:2; 28:41; Isaiah 40:25; Ezekiel 43:7-9; 1 Peter 1:15, 16; Revelation 15:4)*

While holiness is in one sense the unique and exclusive perfection of God, it is capable, under divinely appointed conditions, of being given to persons, places, and things. In the New Testament holiness not only incorporates the concepts of the Old Testament but it also addresses the issue of why we do what we do. God doesn't expect us to always have perfect behavior and never make a mistake, but he does expect us to have perfect motives. In theology this is often called Christian Perfection, Entire Sanctification or Holiness.

My wife and I once had a teenage foster girl that had a shirt she loved to wear that said, "Pobody's Nerfect." If you knew this girl you would certainly agree that she often lived up to her favorite motto! We would all concur that humans have many shortcomings but the Bible makes it clear that God expects us to have perfect and pure motives in life. That means that we are to be led by God's word and the Holy Spirit to always do, or not do, what we believe to be right in the eyes of God. *"The Lord sees not as man sees: man looks on the outward appearance, but the Lord looks on the heart." (1 Samuel 16:7)*

Truth

One of the things that is very evident in our world is that liars are easy to find. I am sure that you have never told a lie but the rest of us certainly have! Some people even make a living of it. (I didn't say politician did I?) It's interesting to note that in the book of Revelation some of the poor souls that find themselves in the lake of fire are "all liars." *(Revelation 21:8)* Kind of makes you want to reconsider your honesty doesn't it?

God can never be misleading, deceptive or dishonest in any way. Any act or any word of revelation by God is an expression of holy love. Truth as a perfection of God indicates that God's analysis of people is based on His perfect knowledge of what a person is and what they can become. God is true and faithful in that He always acts in harmony with His nature. His purposes never waver, and His promises are always kept. *(Exodus 34:6; Numbers 23:19; Deuteronomy 32:4; Psalm 100:5; 146:6; Isaiah 25:1; 1 Corinthians 10:13; 2 Timothy 2:13; Titus 1:2; Revelation 15:3)*

Righteousness - Justice

Throughout the years I have conducted many funerals and memorial services. Remembering a Christian who has died is a blessing. But, there are times when either I don't know if they were a Christian or in some cases it was very clear that they had nothing to do with the Lord. Often in these situations I have had loved ones ask me if I think the deceased person is in heaven. It would be cruel to blurt out, "No, your loved one is burning in hell!" So, I sometimes say, "If there was any way God can get 'George' into heaven, He will do it." The reason I can say that is because I know that God is merciful and just. He never makes a mistake.

In the Old Testament the words Righteous and Justice are taken from the same Hebrew word. To say that God is Righteous or Just is to say that God always is, and does, what is right. In founding and maintaining fellowship with His creation God wills and expresses and establishes what corresponds to His own nature.

In today's culture many people struggle with what is right and wrong. Morality can't simply be based on what is legal and what is not. If that were true then slavery would have been morally right! In order for there to be justice in the world there must be a universal law giver. God in His perfection is the only one who can set the standards of moral being and behavior. *(Exodus 34:6; Deuteronomy 32:4; Psalm 19:9; 89:14; Isaiah 11:5; 45:21; Romans 1:17; Revelation 15:3; 16:5)*

Love

In 1967 the rock group the Beatles recorded a song that said, "All you need is love, all you need is love, all you need is love, love, love is all you need." It had a catchy tune and you couldn't help singing along with it. Now, the Beatles were far from being good theologians but it is true that love is all you need. The problem is that most people don't understand what love is really all about. As a matter of fact, the English language only has one word for love while the Greek New Testament speaks of three kinds of love; friendship love, erotic love and self-giving or commitment love which is the love God has for us.

The Bible simply states, *"God is love." (1 John 4:8)* This does not mean, "Love is God." (That is something the Beatles were confused about.) God's love does not need an object to exist, since it is His very essence. God's love is supremely demonstrated in the life and death of Jesus. (Romans 5:8) God's love always seeks for the best for his creation. The love of God is one of the great realities of the universe, a pillar upon which the hope of the world rests. But it is a personal, intimate thing, too. God does not just love populations, He loves individuals. He loves us all with a mighty love that has no beginning and can have no end.

When speaking about the subject of Love Jesus said, "You therefore must be perfect, as your heavenly Father is perfect." (Matthew 5:48) Also, when Jesus was asked what the greatest commandment was he said, *"You shall love the Lord your God with all your heart and with all your soul and with all your mind. This is the great and first commandment. And a second is like it: You shall love your neighbor as yourself. On these two commandments depend all the Law and the Prophets." (Matthew 22:37-40)* To have the kind of love God requires is only possible when we allow God's perfect love to love through us.

Mercy

A very unattractive woman once went to a painter to have her portrait painted. After spending a considerable amount of time and money she was finally shown the painting. In shock she exclaimed, "That is terrible, I want justice." After looking back and forth at the woman and the painting the distraught artist said, "Lady, you don't need justice, what you need is mercy!"

Mercy is exactly what we need. As the contemporary song says: "If it wasn't for your mercy, if it wasn't for your love, if it wasn't for your kindness how could I stand?" Mercy is an infinite and inexhaustible energy within God to be actively compassionate. *"But God, being rich in mercy, because of the great love with which he loved us, even when we were dead in our trespasses, made us alive together with Christ—by grace you have been saved— and raised us up with him and seated us with him in the heavenly places in Christ Jesus, so that in the coming ages he might show the immeasurable riches of his grace in kindness toward us in Christ Jesus." (Ephesians 2:4-7)*

God's mercy is not a temporary mood but an attribute of God's eternal being. We do not need to be afraid that God will someday cease to be merciful. We also need to remember that God's mercy does not displace God's justice. God's mercy is just. That is one of the reasons why Jesus went to the cross; to pay for our sins. To reject God's mercy is disastrous! When His mercy is despised he will always deal in justice.

A spirit of mercy should also characterize the Christian. *"Speak and so act as those who are to be judged under the law of liberty. For judgment is without mercy to one who has shown no mercy. Mercy triumphs over judgment." (James 2:12-13) (see also: Exodus 34:6-7; Numbers 14:18; Deuteronomy 4:31; Psalm 62:12; 100:5; 103:8; 116:5; 138:8; Lamentations 3:22; Jonah 4:2; Micah 7:18; Romans 8:32; 2 Corinthians 1:3)*

4. The Trinity

One of the most crucial and most misunderstood doctrines in the Bible is the doctrine of the Trinity. This doctrine is so important that it is the major dividing point between true Christians and religious cults that claim to be Christian but really are not. This doctrine is also one of the most difficult to explain because it is beyond physical description. Its incomprehensibility, however, proves nothing but that we are finite beings, and not God. So how do we know it is true? Remember Wesley's quadrilateral? The foundation for what we believe is the Bible. If God's word says it is true then it is, whether we can completely understand it or not. Just because I can't comprehend how my computer works doesn't mean that it doesn't exist!

Cult groups will say that the word "trinity" doesn't occur in Scripture so it isn't true. But neither does the word omnipresence and many other theological words. The absence of these terms doesn't make the theology incorrect. Rather, the language of theology helps to understand doctrines essential to Christian belief and taught by Scripture.

Proof of the Trinity can be found in a remarkable peculiarity in the Hebrew language. The very first word for God in the original Scriptures is Elohim. That this word is plural is certain not only from its form, but also by its often being joined with other words in the plural number. Not only is this word recorded in _Genesis 1:1_ but it also occurs in at least two thousand five hundred other places in the Bible.

The doctrine of there being only one true God is taught throughout the entire Bible. Remember, the Hebrew word "Shema (hear)" stands for the Jewish confession of faith. It is recited daily by the pious: _"Hear, O Israel: The Lord our God, the Lord is one. You shall love the Lord your God with all your heart and with all your soul and with all your might." (Deuteronomy 6:4-5)_ When Abraham and Israel presented the idea of a monotheistic (big word meaning only one God) religion it was shocking to the people of the time. A belief in polytheism (another big word meaning many gods) was common. This is also a problem that the Romans had with Jews and Christians. They were willing to accept their God as one of many but not the only one.

The doctrine of the Trinity is understood by looking at the entire witness of Scripture. The truth of the Trinity is that there are three persons of one substance, power, and eternity – the Father, the Son, and the Holy Spirit.

Plurality of Persons

1. The use of plural pronouns points to the plurality of persons within the Godhead in the Old Testament. God said, _"Let us make man in our image, after our likeness." (Genesis 1:26)_

2. The use of the singular word "name" when referring to God the Father, Son, And Holy Spirit indicates a unity within the three-ness of God. _"Go therefore and make disciples of all nations, baptizing them in the name of the Father and of the Son and of the Holy Spirit." (Matthew 28:19)_

Persons of the Same Essence

Attribute	Father	Son	Holy Spirit
Eternity	Psalm 90:2	John 1:1-2; Revelation 1:8-18	Hebrews 9:14
Power	1 Peter 1:5	2 Corinthians 12:9	Romans 15:19
Omniscience	Jeremiah 17:10	Revelation 2:23	1 Corinthians 2:11
Omnipresence	Jeremiah 23:24	Matthew 18:20	Psalm 139:7-12
Holiness	Revelation 15:4	Acts 3:14	Acts 1:8
Truth	John 7:28	Revelation 3:7	1 John 5:6
Benevolence	Romans 2:4	Ephesians 5:25	Nehemiah 9:20

Equality With Different Roles

Activity	Father	Son	Holy Spirit
Creation of the world	Psalm 102:25	Colossians 1:16	Genesis 1:2 Job 26:13
Creation of mankind	Genesis 2:7	Colossians 1:16	Job 33:4
Baptism of Christ	Matthew 3:17	Matthew 3:16	Matthew 3:16
Death of Christ	Hebrews 9:14	Hebrews 9:14	Hebrews 9:14

Major Heresies Regarding the Trinity

Religion	Father	Son	Holy Spirit
Jehovah's Witnesses (Arianism)	-Only Jehovah is Divine. -Satan created the doctrine of the Trinity.	-Created by Jehovah. -Michael the archangel was Jesus Christ. -No physical resurrection, only spiritual.	-The invisible active force of Almighty God.
Mormonism (Tritheism)	-There are three Gods. -God is a progressive being.	-By obedience and devotion Jesus became a god. -People can also become gods.	-The influence of deity. -He can only be in one place at one time.
New Age	-God is everything. -Everything is God. -Pantheism -Reincarnation	-A person who through many reincarnations became qualified to be a great teacher.	-Channeling Spirit guides
United Pentecostal Church	There is one Person manifesting himself in three different ways. (So was Jesus praying to himself?)		
Unitarianism	The Holy Spirit is an influence, and Jesus Christ was a mere man, the son of Joseph, of high moral excellence, which it is possible for us to equal, or even excel. Human reason and experience should be the final authority in determining spiritual truth.		

Church History Moment
Nicene Creed - AD 325

"We believe in one God, the Father, almighty, maker of all things visible and invisible; And in one Lord Jesus Christ, the son of God, begotten from the Father, only-begotten, that is, from the substance of the Father, God from God, light from light, true God from true God, begotten not made, of one substance from the Father, through Whom all things came into being, things in heaven and things on earth, who because of us men and because of our salvation came down and became incarnate, becoming man, suffered and rose again on the third day, ascended to the heavens, will come to judge the living and the dead; And in the Holy Spirit. But as for those who say, there was a time when he was not, and, before being born he was not, and he came into existence out of nothing, or who assert that the son of God is a different hypostasis or substance, or is subject to change or alteration – these the Catholic and Apostolic Church anathematizes."

5. Errors Concerning the Nature of God

There are a lot of really messed up ideas about God. These range from thinking that God is everything and everything is God (pantheism) down to the sacrilegious view that God is simply another person on the same level as any other human. I remember talking with a man once about salvation. He told me that he and "the man upstairs" had worked out his own salvation. You can't negotiate your own plan of redemption with God Almighty! It's a very dangerous position to be in to tell God what to do. *"Who are you, O man, to answer back to God?" (Romans 9:20)*

On a large scale there are some major religious beliefs about God that are totally contrary to the God of Scripture. A few are listed below.

Pantheism

Ever have the desire to look like a Greek god? Well, according to some people you already do. Pantheism is the view that God is everything and everything is God. This is a fundamental belief of Hinduism. Everything that has ever been, is now, or ever will be, is all a part of God.

Polytheism

Hey, why only have one God when you can have many? That is the view of polytheism. Each god is distinct and has varying powers. They can even get married to each other and sometimes go to war against other gods. Classic polytheism can be seen in the multitude of gods in Greek mythology.

Animism

Ever talk to your plants? If you do I am sure that they don't talk back to you. That would be pretty weird wouldn't it? "Fern, how are you doing today?" "Well, I'm feeling a bit down, could you give me some steer manure?"

The "earth religions" such as Wicca, primitive tribal religions and many native American Indians believe that everything has a "soul" or spirit. This includes animals, plants, rocks, mountains, rivers and so forth. Each spirit is powerful and can help or hurt them, including the souls of the dead, the "ancestors." For thousands of years they deified animals, stars, idols of any kind... and practiced spiritism, witchcraft, divination, astrology using magic, spells, enchantments, superstitions, prayers, amulets, talismans and charms. If they received any supernatural response from their worship or incantations it was not from God but rather from demonic spirits masquerading as a god or spiritual force.

Atheism

"The fool says in his heart, "There is no God." They are corrupt, doing abominable iniquity; there is none who does good." (Psalm 53:1) Enough said!

Now, lets take a look at some important theology regarding the nature of Jesus.

6. Christology

Of particular interest to us is an understanding of who Jesus Christ is. Its important to us because of the central role Jesus makes in our salvation, personal conduct and future. The study of Christology is a vast study that covers the entire subject of who Jesus Christ is and what he has accomplished. For our discussion we will consider two major points. The fact that Jesus Christ was equally man and equally God is of greatest importance. It may be difficult for us to fully comprehend but here again we need to accept the clear teachings of Scripture.

Jesus Christ was truly a human being

Some people find it strange to think that Jesus had to go to the bathroom, had bad breath and needed to eat, drink water and sleep. But the fact remains that every human who has ever lived on the earth has had the same needs and physical issues of every other human being. The Scriptures teach us that Jesus was truly a man. The Bible says that Jesus was born _(Isaiah 9:6; 7:14 & Matthew 1:18-25)_ and calls Jesus the son of man, eighty times. It says he was made flesh, _(John 1:4)_; made of woman, _(Galatians 4:4)_; had the likeness of man, _(Phil. 2:7)_. He grew, _(Luke 2:52)_; was hungry, _(Matthew 4:2)_; got tired, _(John 4:6)_; was tempted, _(Matthew 4:2)_; He sweat, _(Luke 22:44)_; and wept, _(John 11:35)_; was angry and grieved, _(Mark 3:5)_; He died, _(John 19:33)_; and was buried _(John 19:42)_.

Also, all of those Scriptures that speak of his sufferings and death, or indicate weakness, in any sense, prove his real humanity. However, they don't prove him to be a mere man, as some have supposed, neither do they prove him to be an angel or an arch angel as others have supposed; but they prove him to have been a real man, possessed, like other men, of a human body and a human soul.

Jesus Christ is truly God
The heavy weight boxing champion Muhammad Ali was known for his arrogance and used to boast, "I am the greatest!" Once when he was on a plane the flight attendant told him to fasten his seat belt. He said, "Superman don't need no seat belt!" The flight attendant responded with "Superman don't need no airplane either!"

Even though a lot of people act like they think they are God there is only one human being who really was: The Lord Jesus Christ. The Bible is clear in its assertion that Jesus was God in the flesh. The lists of the attributes of Jesus that we discussed on the subject of the Trinity also support the divinity of Christ.

Important Word - Divine: Describes the being of the true God as well as things that come from God and are therefore regarded as sacred and holy.
Some of the Scriptures that directly speak of Jesus as God are: _"In the beginning was the Word, and the Word was with God, and the Word was God." (John 1:1) "Christ, who is God over all, blessed_

forever." (Romans 9:5) "Have this mind among yourselves, which is yours in Christ Jesus, who, though he was in the form of God, did not count equality with God a thing to be grasped, but emptied himself, by taking the form of a servant, being born in the likeness of men." (Philippians 2:5-6) When confronted with the risen Christ, Thomas responded, "My Lord and my God!" (John 20:28). Jesus did not rebuke him for his "mistake" but rather said that others would be blessed for believing that truth by faith and not sight.

In the Bible worship is strictly limited to God alone. Jesus was quoting from the book of _Deuteronomy (chapter 6)_ when he said in _Luke 4:8 "The Scriptures say, 'You must worship the Lord your God and serve only him.'"_ If Jesus is not God, as some claim, then why does the Bible teach that Jesus is deserving of, and accepts worship? _(Matthew 2:11; 14:33; Luke 24:52; Hebrews 1:6)_ If worshiping Jesus is wrong then there is a major problem in heaven: _"Then I looked, and I heard around the throne and the living creatures and the elders the voice of many angels, numbering myriads of myriads and thousands of thousands, saying with a loud voice, 'Worthy is the Lamb who was slain, to receive power and wealth and wisdom and might and honor and glory and blessing!' And I heard every creature in heaven and on earth and under the earth and in the sea, and all that is in them, saying, 'To him who sits on the throne and to the Lamb be blessing and honor and glory and might forever and ever!' And the four living creatures said, 'Amen!' and the elders fell down and worshiped." (Revelation 5:11-14)_

7. Pneumatology

The first thing that needs to be clear from the beginning is that the Holy Spirit is not an "it." This is a common mistake made by many. The Holy Spirit is a person and should be addressed as such. Besides the attributes of the Holy Spirit already addressed, the following are some aspects of His work and personality.

Personality of the Holy Spirit	
Baptizing in His Name	Matthew 28:19
Giving Love	Romans 15:30
Fellowship	2 Corinthians 13:14
Feels Sorrow	Ephesians 4:30

An Advocate for Christians	*John 14:16*
Teacher	*John 14:26 & 1 John 2:27*
Calling & Sending	*Acts 13:2-4*
Prays for Christians	*Romans 8:26*
Gives Conviction for Sin	*John 16:8*
Gives Eternal Life	*John 6:63 & Titus 3:4-5*
Affirms our Salvation	*Romans 8:16*
Makes us Holy	*1 Corinthians 6:11*
Inspires Prophets	*2 Peter 1:20-21*
Gives Spiritual Gifts	*1 Corinthians 12*
Produces Righteous Fruit	*Galatians 5:22*

One of the most baffling and confusing doctrines of the Bible relates to the Holy Spirit. It is known as the "unforgivable sin." Reference to it is found in *Mark 3* and *Matthew 12* where Jesus was once again being disrespected by the religious leaders. Jesus said, *"Therefore I tell you, every sin and blasphemy will be forgiven people, but the blasphemy against the Spirit will not be forgiven. And whoever speaks a word against the Son of Man will be forgiven, but whoever speaks against the Holy Spirit will not be forgiven, either in this age or in the age to come." (Matthew 12:31-32)*

Just what is the unforgivable sin? Among other things, blasphemy is defiant irreverence for God. It is extremely dangerous to disrespect God. In the context of the above Scripture the religious leaders were accusing Jesus of driving out evil spirits with the assistance of satan. You can't do much worse than call God satan! This blasphemy has to do with someone accusing the Lord Jesus as being demon-possessed instead of being Spirit-filled. It is attributing evil to God.

The unforgivable sin is when a person has a continual heart-attitude of disrespect, unbelief and non-repentance. Deliberate, ongoing rejection of the work of the Holy Spirit is blasphemy because it is rejection of God himself. True Christians don't need to worry that they have somehow committed the unforgivable sin since their attitude is not one of rejection and defiance but rather one of love and acceptance.

Section 3
Christian Apologetics

First of all, apologetics is not the study of how to apologize! That would be good to know but it is not the focus of this section. Christian Apologetics is the art and science of proving the truth of Christianity. It is art in the sense that good skill at argumentation, logic and reason need to be used in persuading the truth of God, His word and His creation. It is science in that the truth of the natural world always points to a creator. *"The wrath of God is revealed from heaven against all ungodliness and unrighteousness of men, who by their unrighteousness suppress the truth. For what can be known about God is plain to them, because God has shown it to them. For his invisible attributes, namely, his eternal power and divine nature, have been clearly perceived, ever since the creation of the world, in the things that have been made. So they are without excuse." (Romans 1:18-20)*

Atheistic philosophy attempts to teach unproven theories of evolution as fact. But when carefully considered, that approach requires much more faith and outlandish speculation than Christianity has ever had! For the most part, modern education and non-Christian media continuously assert that we evolved from some lower life form. They are unable to say where that life form came from but they continue to insist on ideas that clearly fail to stand the test of logic and empirical evidence. When they are confronted with contradictions in the supposed evidence they often just add more years to their theory hoping that it will somehow convince a person to believe a deception. Think about it for a minute, how can adding more years make a non-object into an object. Or, how many years are needed to make life out of non-life?

Three Approaches
There are many different approaches to understanding the proof of God's existence and the reality of time, space and matter. We will briefly look at three of the most widely used.

1. Philosophy
Important Word
Metaphysics: The branch of philosophy that concerns itself with questions about the nature of ultimate reality. Included are: the nature of existence, the nature of time and space, the relationship of mind and body, the reality of abstract objects and the existence of God.

Cosmological Argument
Everything that exists in the physical realm must have had a cause. You would think that no one would argue against this truth but amazingly, the atheistic proponents of evolution state that time and matter always existed! There is no way logically that this could be true. It is forcing intellectual suicide in an attempt to explain something that is easily understood by the truth of God, who is outside of the physical realm, and His creation.

Law of Non-contradiction
Aristotle said that "one cannot say of something that it is and that it is not in the same respect and at the same time." Another way to say this is that "A" cannot be "A" and "non-A" at the same time and in the same relationship. Something can be "A" and "B" at the same time but not in the same relationship. I can be a father (A) and a son (B) at the same time, but not in the same relationship. I cannot

be my own father, even if I "identify" as such. Simply stated, in the context of being, something cannot create itself.

For most of us this makes perfect sense. But for those who reject Divine Creation their only option is to reject the Law of Non-contradiction. I like what the ancient philosopher Avicenna said: "Anyone who denies the law of non-contradiction should be beaten and burned until he admits that to be beaten is not the same as not to be beaten, and to be burned is not the same as not to be burned."

In Christian theology this law would teach, among other things, that one cannot be both the created and the creator. Nothing comes from nothing. There must be a non-created source... God.

Note: If you exclude the spiritual and only believe in the natural world then you have to conclude that even "nothing" is something and had to come from somewhere.

To say this in another way:
1. Every finite and contingent being has a cause.
2. A causal loop cannot exist. Something cannot create itself.
3. A causal chain cannot be of infinite length. One cannot go further back in time to come to a materialistic time/space beginning that independently exists.
4. Therefore, an Intelligent First Cause (or something that is not an effect) must exist.

Teleological Argument
The universe has design and fine-tuning. It is amazing to me that anyone with any intelligence at all can look at everything that naturally exists and think it all came together by chance. It is clear that there is a definite design to the natural order of things. Beauty and creativity don't just happen. It takes an active, precise mind to put complex things together in a way that they function properly on a consistent basis. As I stated before, everything we see in nature clearly points to a divine creator.

Objective moral values

There are universal moral values that could only come from a moral being. Even though there are few exceptions, throughout history and across all cultural boundaries certain moral standards have been accepted as right or wrong. Even those who reject a moral lawgiver claim that there are universal "human rights" that should be recognized. If one were to follow the logical progression of evolutionary thought then the rule of "survival of the fittest" would be the standard for establishing moral conduct. This would mean that if you are able to subdue or destroy someone or something for your own benefit then that would be acceptable.

Historical facts concerning Jesus

From a historical perspective the proof of Jesus' resurrection far surpasses any logical refutation. Much of recorded history has been manipulated or re-written to promote a certain political or philosophical agenda so one needs to be careful in accepting the arguments of biased "historians." Historical evidence needs to be obtained from as many original sources as possible and those sources need to be evaluated carefully to insure accuracy. History should be allowed to speak for itself rather than distorted to convince naive people to accept faulty conclusions. There is more accurate historical proof that Jesus rose from the dead than there is that George Washington ever existed and yet many people quickly dismiss the resurrection but readily accept the reality of George Washington!

God can be personally known

True believers have a personal relationship with God. If you are a genuine Christian you know of times when it is very clear that God's Spirit is communicating with your spirit. For me this is often during times of prayer but especially during worship. It is a supernatural experience that cannot be explained or demonstrated in an empirical way but is very real to the person who knows God. *"For you did not receive the spirit of slavery to fall back into fear, but you have received the Spirit of adoption as sons, by whom we cry, 'Abba! Father!' The Spirit himself bears witness with our spirit that we are children of God." (Romans 8:15-16)*

2. Prophecy

What would you say if I told you that at exactly 3:00 pm tomorrow a bug would fly up your nose? You'd probably laugh. But what if it really happened just like I said? And then what would you do if I gave you a long list of predictions that all came true to the letter? You would both be amazed and probably a bit freaked out!

Over the years a lot of people have made predictions about the future and some have come true but most have not. Usually the ones that come true are generalizations that anyone could make. There is one book, however, that has made hundreds of predictions that have all happened exactly as foretold. You guessed it, the Bible. While some of the Biblical prophecies are general in nature there are many that are very specific. This is the only book in the history of the world that has always been 100% accurate. Let's look at a couple of specific examples.

Cyrus

At about 700 B.C. the prophet Isaiah wrote that a king would give a command for Jerusalem to be rebuilt and that the temple foundation should be laid. God speaking: "Cyrus, 'He is my shepherd, and he shall fulfill all my purpose'; saying of Jerusalem, 'She shall be built,' and of the temple, 'Your foundation shall be laid.'" (Isaiah 44:28)

When Isaiah gave the prophecy the city of Jerusalem was fully built and the entire temple was standing. It wasn't until more than one hundred years later, in 586 B.C, that the city and Temple were destroyed by King Nebuchadnezzar.

After Jerusalem was conquered by the Babylonians, it was later taken by a Persian king by the name of Cyrus who gave the order to rebuild the Temple in Jerusalem. This was around 160 years after the prophecy of Isaiah!

Daniel's Seventy Weeks

Perhaps one the most incredible prophecies in the Bible is what is known as Daniel's Seventy Weeks. The Bible predicts to the day when Jesus would ride into Jerusalem declaring himself as King.

1. In Daniel 9:24-27 the Bible predicts that at the end of 69 seven-year periods (weeks of years equaling 483 years) the Messiah will enter Jerusalem.

2. The starting point of the 69 weeks is the decree to restore and rebuild Jerusalem. This occurred when Artaxerxes gave the command in the book of Nehemiah chapter two. This would be Nisan 1,444 B.C.

3. In the Bible the only years whose length is given are 360 days. Twelve months of 30 days each. (Genesis 7, Revelation 11-13) Multiplying the 69 weeks by seven years for each week by 360 days gives a total of 173,880 days. The difference between 444 B.C. and A.D. 33 then is 476 solar years. By multiplying 476 by 365.24219879, or by 365 days, 5 hours, 48 minutes, 45.975 seconds, one comes to 173,855 days. This leaves only 25 days to be accounted for between 444 B.C. and A.D. 33. By adding the 25 days to March 5 (of 444 B.C.), one comes to March 30 (of A.D. 33) which was Nisan 10 in A.D. 33.

4. The final event of the 69 weeks is the presentation of Christ to Israel as the Messiah as predicted in Zechariah 9:9. This happened on Monday, March 30, A.D. 33 when Jesus rode the donkey into Jerusalem. During the time of Christ kings were often led into cities on donkeys proclaiming their royalty and victory over enemies.

3. Science

One of the stupid things people say is that they don't believe in religion; they believe in science. Usually these are people who have very little knowledge of both. Contrary to what people think, every scientific fact (not theory which is assumed by many to be fact) supports the belief in God. Scientific studies in DNA illustrate that truth.

DNA is known as the "building Blocks of life."

-Every person has unique DNA

-The sequence of DNA development is not simple, and it's not random:

1. Amino acids need to be selected with proper orientation. Life specific amino acids must be sorted with incorrect ones rejected.

2. Correct amino acids need to be bonded into short chains.

3. Hundreds of short chains need to be bonded to specified length.

4. Chains with "sensible" order must be selected.

Scientists have estimated that the probability of all of these steps to randomly occur to form the simplest living cell is 1 in $10^{100,000,000,000}$ chances, (like winning 1.4 million lotteries in a row!). And we still have to ask, "Where did the living cell come from in the beginning?" Many scientists have determined that anything whose probability is less than one chance in 50,000,000 is beyond reason and considered impossible. Therefore: Reasonable science has concluded that the formation of DNA by chance is impossible.

Science and the Bible		
Fact	Biblical Statement	Scientific Confirmation
General Relativity (Time, Space, Matter all had a beginning)	1400 – *Genesis 1:1* "*In the beginning God created the heavens and the earth.*"	1916 Einstein
1st law of Thermodynamics (Matter and energy cannot be created or destroyed)	1400 B.C. – Genesis 2:2 "*On the seventh day God had finished his work of creation…*"	1842 Joule, Mayer

2nd law of Thermodynamics (Entropy – things tend to move from a state of order to disorder)	1000 B.C. – _Psalm 102:25-26 "Long ago you laid the foundation of the earth and made the heavens with your hands. They will perish, but you remain forever; they will wear out like old clothing..."_	1850 Clausius
Hydrologic Cycle defined	2000 B.C. – _Job 36:27-28 "For he draws up the drops of water, They distill rain from the mist, Which the clouds pour down, They drip upon man abundantly."_	1700s Perrault and Mariotte

Section 4
Cosmology

Is this the theology of hair styling? If that's what you're looking for, sorry. It has nothing to do with hair styling and makeup (cosmetology). Cosmology is the study that deals with the origin and nature of the universe as an orderly system. Whether you believe in a Divine Creator, or not, is foundational to everything about you. Your whole value system is determined by your view of where you came from. If you believe that you evolved from some pond scum or are a descendant of a monkey then it is not surprising that your rule for conduct is usually governed by pleasure and selfishness. You only have to answer to yourself. If, on the other hand, you believe that God made everything then you are accountable to Him.

There are many theories about how the universe began. Some are pretty weird like an ancient Chinese story of creation. People actually believed that the universe began with a cosmic egg (No one knows where the egg came from.). Inside the egg was a chaotic mixture of yin/yang, male/female, cold/heat etc. From the egg a giant by the name of Phan Ku was born. He separated the earth and the sky. He grew ten feet taller every day, raising the sky above the earth by that distance. He also created the stars and planets. On earth he carved out the mountains and valleys with a huge chisel and mallet. When he died, the fleas in his hair became human beings. I don't know, would you rather be a flea or a monkey, or why not a cockroach, they seem to be impossible to kill? Ever see the movie WALL-E?

For anyone that thinks logically, many theories are easily dismissed but there are others that, even though they are wrong, they are believed by many people. A few of the major non-Biblical theories of the origin of the universe are listed here.

1. Non-Biblical Theories of the Origin of the Universe

The Physical or Materialistic Theory
This theory of the origin of the universe presupposes the eternity of matter. The hypothesis of spontaneous generation is substituted for God as the Builder of the universe. It is amazing how many people believe this theory as fact when it clearly violates at least two scientific principles that we discussed earlier. First, this theory violates the scientific law of Cause and Effect that states that for every effect there must be a cause. It also violates the Law of Non-contradiction.

The Pantheistic Theory
The world was neither created nor fashioned out of pre-existent material, but is to be regarded as an extension of the divine substance. God is everything and everything is God. This view is the basis for the Hindu religion as well as some other crazy ideas. In addition to the fact that it doesn't address the beginning of all things it also denies the distinct personality and attributes of God and fails to admit human freedom and immorality. This view also means that you need to be very careful because if you aren't good enough in this life you might be reincarnated into that cockroach we were talking about! That's why in India you don't want to eat cows since you might be eating your great grandmother!

The Theory of Natural Evolution
Naturalistic evolution, the idea that current life evolved from a lower form, instead of solving the problem of creation, merely pushes it back farther and farther in time. The question of origin remains unanswered. Where did it all come from in the first place? Also, the issues regarding complexity are ignored.

Natural Evolution breaks down at three vital points	**1.** It has not been able to bridge the chasm between the inanimate and the animate. **2.** It cannot pass from the diffused life of the vegetable realm to the conscious, somatic life of the animal kingdom. **3.** It cannot span the gap from the somatic life of animals to the rational, self-conscious, spiritual life of people.

2. The Theory of Continuous Creation

This view is generally held by theistic evolutionists. Theistic evolutionists believe that organic development is due, not to materialistic forces, but to divine power working with the organism. It basically teaches that God did create everything but he did it through evolution. This view obviously contradicts the Bible including the clear teaching of the completion of Creation in six days. *(Genesis 1-2)*

3. Important Points Concerning the Biblical Doctrine of Creation

Creation may be defined as the free act of God by which He brought into existence the universe and all that it contains, without the use of preexistent materials. *"He is the image of the invisible God, the firstborn of all creation. For by him all things were created, in heaven and on earth, visible and invisible, whether thrones or dominions or rulers or authorities—all things were created through him and for him." (Colossians 1:15-16)*

1. The world, including mankind was not created to meet a need or a deficiency in God, for the divine nature has no inherent needs. *"The God who made the world and everything in it, being Lord of heaven and earth, does not live in temples made by man, nor is he served by human hands, as though he needed anything, since he himself gives to all mankind life and breath and everything." (Acts 17:24-25)*

2. The world has a distinct and separate existence. The world should not be regarded as part of God or as God himself (pantheism). Yet the world is absolutely dependent on God and must be upheld from moment to moment by His almighty power. *"He is before all things, and in him all things hold together." (Colossians 1:17)*

3. The world was created with time rather than in time. Creation was by the simple command or word of God. This is a very important point. We are bound by time and space which were both created. People who do not believe in a Divine Creator can not explain where and when the beginning of time happened. (see *Genesis Chapter One*)

4. Adam and Eve are the only people who never had to go through those difficult teenage years. The first man and woman were created in a mature state. God also created the world in a mature state. What that means is that at the time of creation God made everything as though it had existed for many years. Yes, we can answer the question, "What came first, the chicken or the egg." Clearly the bird came first. In addition, God did not create a flat earth with no mountains or valleys. He also did not create a bunch of elements that eventually grew into trees and plants. Why does the universe look so old? Because that is the way God created it. He created a mature earth.

5. In the Old Testament the word for day could also mean a "period of time," however since God is Omnipotent it was no problem for him to create the world in six literal days. If you think the "days" are long periods of time you quickly run into a problem. The trees and plants are created on the third day but insects needed for pollination are not created until day six. If each day was really hundreds or thousands of years then the trees and plants would not have survived.

6. To try to prove the creation of the world in a scientific way with the Bible is really kind of foolish. The Scripture is not a scientific textbook. There are, however, no conflicts with the true facts of science. If genuine science encounters the Bible at all, it always agrees with, and never contradicts, it. The Hebrew mind (the Old Testament) was basically concerned with what happened. It was enough for them to know that God created everything. The Greek mind (the New Testament) is more concerned with why things happen. The modern Scientific mind wants to know the specifics on how it happened. The problem, as I stated before, is that too often scientific theories, many which have very little actual fact, are taught and accepted as truth and not as theory.

Section 5
Humankind

Every person who has ever existed has descended from Adam and Eve. That's right, you are even related to that disgusting person you saw at the store this week. All of humankind have a oneness of nature that is taught in the Bible. *(Genesis 1:27-28; 2:7, 18, 21-24; 3:20; Malachi 2:10; Acts 17:26; Romans 5:12; I Corinthians 15:22, 45.)*

Humans are complex beings comprised of a body, a soul and a spirit. The body is mortal, made from the dust of the earth, while the spirit is immortal, continuing to live after it leaves the body in a state of conscious existence. *(Ecclesiastes 3:21; I Kings 17:21-22; Luke 8:55; 16:22-23; 23:43; Matthew 10:28; 22:32; Acts 7:59; II Corinthians 5:8; Philippians 1:23; Revelation 6:9-11; 14:13)*

The Apostle Paul speaks of the soul, in *I Thessalonians 5:23 "Now may the God of peace himself sanctify you completely, and may your whole spirit and soul and body be kept blameless at the coming of our Lord Jesus Christ."* Traditionally the soul has been understood as consisting of the mind, will, and emotions. The spirit is that part of our nature that enables us to encounter the Spirit of God. In the unbeliever it is dead and cannot connect with God.

"Now we have received not the spirit of the world, but the Spirit who is from God, that we might understand the things freely given us by God. And we impart this in words not taught by human wisdom but

taught by the Spirit, interpreting spiritual truths to those who are spiritual. The natural person does not accept the things of the Spirit of God, for they are folly to him, and he is not able to understand them because they are spiritually discerned." 1 Corinthians 2:12-14.

Humans were originally made to be morally pure but that didn't last very long. In order for them to be moral they needed to be able to be immoral. And, as you know they accepted the invitation of satan and chose to reject the standards of God. This is clearly evident in today's rampant immorality. Sadly, this rejection of biblical morality is becoming acceptable as normal human behavior and Christian morality is belittled or repudiated as being outdated.

The first sin of Adam and Eve changed their whole moral nature, from a holy to a sinful state. As a result, the sinful nature has passed on down through generation to generation to include everyone who has ever lived. *(Romans 5:12; 1 Corinthians 15:22; Ephesians 2:3, 5; Job 15:14; Psalm 14:2-3; Psalm 51:5; Psalm 58:3)*

Even though we inherited the nature to sin we can't blame it all on mom and dad. The Bible teaches us that each of us are responsible for our own sin. *(Deuteronomy 24:16; 2 Kings 14:6; Proverbs 11:19; Ezekiel 18:4, 20; Jeremiah 31:30; Romans 1:20-21; John 3:19-20)*

Section 6
Soteriology

Soteriology is a fancy word for the whole study of the doctrine of salvation. Without God's plan of salvation we would all be toast. Well, not in the literal sense but we would certainly be "toasted" in hell! Thankfully, even though our sinful behavior deserves to be punished, God in his love has made a way for us to escape judgment. _"While we were still weak, at the right time Christ died for the ungodly. For one will scarcely die for a righteous person— though perhaps for a good person one would dare even to die— but God shows his love for us in that while we were still sinners, Christ died for us. Since, therefore, we have now been justified by his blood, much more shall we be saved by him from the wrath of God." (Romans 5:6-9)_

In the study of salvation there are some very important terms that need to be understood. Sometimes people use words that mean different things to different people. When I was growing up the word "coke" was used for any soft drink. You could go to the hamburger joint and order an orange "coke." In the deep south of the United

States "coke" is still used to describe any type of soft drink. So when we talk about theology what do certain words mean to you? What does it mean when someone says to you that you must be born again and sanctified through the blood of Christ? For someone who doesn't know "Christianese" it can soon become pretty confusing.

1. Important Terms Regarding Salvation

Repentance
Without Repentance there is no forgiveness. A lot of people think that salvation is easy. Just say a little prayer in the back of a pamphlet and presto change-o you're saved. That kind of attitude misses a very important point. Both John the Baptist and Jesus preached repentance as a basic condition of entrance into the kingdom of God! *"In those days John the Baptist came preaching in the wilderness of Judea, 'Repent, for the kingdom of heaven is at hand.'" (Matthew 3:1-2) "Bear fruit in keeping with repentance." (Matthew 3:8) "From that time Jesus began to preach, saying, 'Repent, for the kingdom of heaven is at hand.'" (Matthew 4:17) " I tell you; but unless you repent, you will all likewise perish." (Luke 13:3)*

Intellectual Repentance
The sinner comes unto "the Knowledge of sin." *"Through the law comes knowledge of sin." (Romans 3:20)*

Emotional Repentance
A genuine sorrow for sin. *"For godly grief produces a repentance that leads to salvation without regret, whereas worldly grief produces death." (2 Corinthians 7:10)*

Volitional Repentance
In the Bible repentance means to understand we are sinners, to have sorrow for those sins and to go in the opposite direction of sin. A change of the will and purpose is essential. True repentance includes a turning away from sin and a turning toward God. *"The times of ignorance God overlooked, but now he commands all people everywhere to repent." (Acts 17:30)*

Saving Faith

Saving faith is personal trust and acceptance of the Lord Jesus Christ. A trust and faith so genuine that it results in good works and obedience to God's Word.

"What good is it, my brothers, if someone says he has faith but does not have works? Can that faith save him? If a brother or sister is poorly clothed and lacking in daily food, and one of you says to them, 'Go in peace, be warmed and filled,' without giving them the things needed for the body, what good is that? So also faith by itself, if it does not have works, is dead. But someone will say, 'You have faith and I have works.' Show me your faith apart from your works, and I will show you my faith by my works. You believe that God is one; you do well. Even the demons believe—and shudder!" (James 2:14-19)

Conversion

The term conversion is used to describe what happens when one turns away from sin and accepts Jesus into their life. In the Bible this is referred to as becoming "born again." When I was a Prison Chaplain I once had a Corrections Officer come to me and tell me about someone who she thought was an idiot. She said he was one of those "born again" types. I patiently informed her that I was one too! After all, that is what Jesus said you must become if you want to have eternal life! *"Jesus answered him, "Truly, truly, I say to you, unless one is born again he cannot see the kingdom of God.""* *(John 3:3)* So who's the real idiot?

Salvation

There are true Christians in every genuine Christian denomination. An "Evangelical Christian" is a person who believes in the biblical truth that an individual must personally accept Christ as their Savior. They are also usually socially conservative and hold the Bible in very high esteem. But what does it mean to "accept Christ as your Savior?" The answer to the question, "What is required for salvation" has been debated, sometimes violently, ever since the time of Christ. Is it baptism that saves a person? How about church membership? Can you earn your way to salvation? Can reading a little prayer in the back of a booklet, or responding to an emotional appeal during a religious service produce genuine conversion? Can simply calling yourself a Christian be enough? Do you have anything to do with it at all or is is all up to God's choosing?

Repentance (See also previous discussion)

I think that sometimes people are given a false idea of what it means to be a Christian that can even lead to a false sense of spiritual security. For one thing, the concept of repentance is often totally ignored. Some Christians, preachers and churches are so fearful of offending anyone that they teach an easy salvation that is really no salvation at all! This kind of teaching has not only led to false security but has also resulted in wide-spread moral decline. Both John the Baptist and Jesus emphasized the importance of repentance. Remember the Scripture: *"In those days John the Baptist came preaching in the wilderness of Judea, 'Repent, for the kingdom of heaven is at hand.'" (Matthew 3:1-2) "Bear fruit in keeping with repentance." (Matthew 3:8) "From that time Jesus began to preach, saying, 'Repent, for the kingdom of heaven is at hand.'" (Matthew 4:17) "I tell you; but unless you repent, you will all likewise perish." (Luke 13:3)*

So, what does repentance mean? Very simply it means to turn and go in the opposite direction. It includes a sorrow for sins committed against God and a desire and determination to live a life pleasing to Him. *"For godly grief produces a repentance that leads to salvation without regret, whereas worldly grief produces death." (2 Corinthians 7:10)*

The Bible clearly teaches that unless a person changes their attitude and behavior regarding sin then they will not inherit eternal life. You cannot live in continuous sin and expect to go to heaven when you die. It is also important to have a biblical understanding of what sin is. Basically it is a rebellion against the absolute and moral standards of God. Look at *Galatians 5:19-21* which is written to Christians: *"Now the works of the flesh are evident: sexual immorality, impurity, sensuality, idolatry, sorcery, enmity, strife, jealousy, fits of anger, rivalries, dissensions, divisions, envy, drunkenness, orgies, and things like these. I warn you, as I warned you before, that those who do such things will not inherit the kingdom of God."*

2. Important Scripture Relating to Salvation

If you were to ask someone what they would desire more than anything else in the world you would get a lot of answers. Many would say, "I want all the money I could ever spend." A good many would never think of things beyond this world. Most people are so focused on the here and now that they miss the clearly most important thing facing us, our eternal destiny.

When we are a kid we love to get presents, but as we grow older we find more joy in giving than receiving. For most of us we like to give gifts to our friends and family. How many times have we searched high and low for that perfect gift but we are hesitant to share our faith in the Lord? The most important thing we can ever do for someone else is to lead them to Christ.

I once had a friend that I was helping to learn how to bring someone else to the Lord. We were talking with a young man who said he wanted to become a Christian. I had my friend lead him in prayer to accept Christ's forgiveness. During the prayer my friend burst out laughing when the nervous new believer prayed, "Lord I ask me into your heart." Well, the guy did accept the Lord but I told my friend that he might want to be a bit more sensitive in the future.

I have found that one of the best ways to help someone discover salvation is by using the Bible. I either take them through the Bible and show them the passages or I quote them from memory. We know that God has said that His word is powerful and will accomplish what needs to be done. Your own wit and wisdom and gifts at persuasion may be helpful but they are insignificant compared to God's word.

"For as the rain and the snow come down from heaven and do not return there but water the earth, making it bring forth and sprout, giving seed to the sower and bread to the eater, so shall my word be that goes out from my mouth; it shall not return to me empty, but it shall accomplish that which I purpose, and shall succeed in the thing for which I sent it." (Isaiah 55:10-11)

The following are verses that you should memorize if you want to be effective in personal evangelism. You should also be able to clearly and thoroughly explain each of the verses.

1. _Romans 3:23 "All have sinned and fall short of the glory of God."_
2. _Romans 6:23 "The wages of sin is death, but the free gift of God is eternal life in Christ Jesus our Lord."_
3. _John 3:16 "God so loved the world, that he gave his only Son, that whoever believes in him should not perish but have eternal life."_
4. _John 10:10 Jesus said: "I came that they may have life and have it abundantly."_
5. _Romans 10:9 "If you confess with your mouth that Jesus is Lord and believe in your heart that God raised him from the dead, you will be saved."_
6. _Mark 1:15 "The time is fulfilled, and the kingdom of God is at hand; repent and believe in the gospel."_
7. _1 John 1:9 "If we confess our sins, he is faithful and just to forgive us our sins and to cleanse us from all unrighteousness."_
8. _John 1:12 "To all who did receive him, who believed in his name, he gave the right to become children of God."_

3. A Dangerous Doctrine

Most evangelicals believe pretty much the same things but there is one doctrine that can be very dangerous and divisive. That is what is commonly called the "Doctrine of Eternal Security." The basic issue surrounding this doctrine is the question as to whether or not a person can "loose" their salvation after once accepting Christ.

Even though there were various views throughout church history it really came to a head during the protestant reformation. In the 1500s a French theologian by the name of John Calvin developed five points he considered essential regarding salvation. His views were strongly debated among scholars in his day and ever since. Chief among those who opposed his views was the Dutch university professor Jacobus Arminius and his followers known as the Remonstrants. The word remonstrant means: "vigorously objecting or opposing."

A biblical understanding of this doctrine is critical. Once when I was a youth pastor in the Seattle area I had a girl visit my youth group who was from another church. She was living with her boyfriend but she told me she was still going to heaven because her pastor told her that once she accepted Christ she would go to heaven no matter what, even if she lived a life of continual sin. I was very concerned for her and others like her because what I read in the Bible does not support that position. Over the years I have studied and debated this doctrine extensively with pastors, university professors and other theologians and none of their arguments could stand up against the clear teachings of Scripture. I feel that a careful study of Scripture will support the doctrine of Arminianism. (For an in-depth look at this doctrine see the Appendix of this book)

The following chart briefly discusses John Calvin's TULIP along with some of the views of traditional Arminianism.

The Five Points of Calvinism and Arminianism		
TULIP	**Calvinism** "God has determined in Himself what He would have become of every individual of mankind, for they are not all created with a similar destiny; but eternal life is foreordained for some, and eternal damnation for others." John Calvin	**Arminianism** *"For God so loved the world, that he gave his only Son, that whoever believes in him should not perish but have eternal life." John 3:16* *"The Lord is not slow to fulfill his promise as some count slowness, but is patient toward you, not wishing that any should perish, but that all should reach repentance." 2 Peter 3:9*
	Total Depravity	**Free Will**
T	Because of the fall, man is unable of himself to believe the Gospel. He does not have a free will. He cannot choose good over evil in the spiritual realm.	Although human nature was seriously affected by the fall, God has given all people a free will to choose for or against God. The ability to choose is granted by God's **Prevenient Grace** (The Grace that goes before salvation enabling all who will, to believe).
	Unconditional Election	**Conditional Election**
U	God chose certain individuals to salvation and certain individuals to damnation before the foundation of the world. Those God chose will be saved and those God rejected will be lost.	The elect of God are those who by their free will have responded to the universal call of God to believe in Christ for salvation.

L	Limited Atonement	General Atonement
	Christ's redeeming work was intended to save only the elect.	Christ's redeeming work made it possible for anyone to be saved.
I	Irresistible Grace	God's Grace can be resisted
	The Holy Spirit extends to the elect a special inward call that inevitably brings them to salvation.	The Holy Spirit brings all who are willing, to a saving faith in Christ.
P	Perseverance of the Saints	Conditional Salvation
	Once a person is saved they will remain so no matter what they do in this life.	Even after salvation one maintains their free will and can resist the Holy Spirit and reject Christ, resulting in a forfeiture of their salvation.

4. Conditional Salvation

We are saved by the grace of God but the application of the grace of God is contingent upon our continual relationship with Christ through the work of the Holy Spirit. Salvation is conditional. God does not give us a license to sin. *"If we say we have fellowship with him while we walk in darkness, we lie and do not practice the truth. But if we walk in the light, as he is in the light, we have fellowship with one another, and the blood of Jesus his Son cleanses us from all sin." 1 John 1:6-7*

There are many Scriptures that teach conditional salvation and this is such an important subject that I have listed a few of them below. *Luke 8:11-15*
"Now the parable is this: The seed is the word of God. The ones along the path are those who have heard; then the devil comes and takes away the word from their hearts, so that they may not believe and be saved. And the ones on the rock are those who, when they hear the word, receive it with joy. But these have no root; they believe for a while, and in time of testing fall away. And as for what fell among the thorns, they are those who hear, but as they go on their way they are choked by the cares and riches and pleasures of life, and their fruit does not mature. As for that in the good soil, they are those who, hearing the word, hold it fast in an honest and good heart, and bear fruit with patience."

In this parable four different types of people are mentioned. The first group never become Christians but the last three are believers. The last two remain steadfast in their faith but the second one has a serious problem. There is no doubt that at first the second group accepts Christ but they "fall away." It clearly says that they are believers. These are not people who "were never really Christians" as some churches teach. To say that someone who does not remain in the faith was never really saved in the first place is to create "eternal insecurity!" How do you know that you will persevere? Maybe you're not really a Christian after all! Fortunately the Lord doesn't leave us struggling with doubt and fear. God's word affirms in _1 John 5:13 "I write these things to you who believe in the name of the Son of God, that you may know that you have eternal life."_ You notice He doesn't say, "hope" you have eternal life, or "got a good chance" at having eternal life. The idea that if you quit serving the Lord then that shows that you were never saved in the first place is a dangerous doctrine and has absolutely no scriptural support.

Matthew 24:9-13
"Then they will deliver you up to tribulation and put you to death, and you will be hated by all nations for my name's sake. And then many will fall away and betray one another and hate one another. And many false prophets will arise and lead many astray. And because lawlessness will be increased, the love of many will grow cold. But the one who endures to the end will be saved."

In these verses Jesus teaches that in the last days there will be those who turn away from Him and quit following Him. His warning is clear: you must remain faithful to the end! How could you turn away from the Lord if you were never a believer in the first place?

Hebrews 3:12-14
"Take care, brothers, lest there be in any of you an evil, unbelieving heart, leading you to fall away from the living God. But exhort one another every day, as long as it is called "today," that none of you may be hardened by the deceitfulness of sin. For we have come to share in Christ, if indeed we hold our original confidence firm to the end."

"If" is a small word but it has a huge impact on this verse. Sharing in all that belongs to Christ is contingent upon remaining faithful to Him. The warning in this passage is to be very careful against being deceived and turning away from the faith. This warning is clearly to people who are already Christians. No where are unbelievers called "brothers and sisters." This concern would have no meaning at all if it were not possible for someone to loose their relationship with Christ. There is nothing in Scripture that supports the idea that you can be "out of fellowship" with the Lord here on earth and be "in fellowship" once you die.

2 Peter 2:20-21
"For if, after they have escaped the defilements of the world through the knowledge of our Lord and Savior Jesus Christ, they are again entangled in them and overcome, the last state has become worse for them than the first. For it would have been better for them never to have known the way of righteousness than after knowing it to turn back from the holy commandment delivered to them."

If one eventually made it to heaven while being "out of fellowship" on earth then that would certainly be better than not believing in the first place! The warning in this Scripture clearly teaches that to know the Lord and then fall away puts a person in a very dangerous position. They no longer have salvation. As a matter of fact, after knowing the Lord their rejection of the knowledge of God hardens their hearts and makes it less likely that they will again come back to where they need to be spiritually.

Romans 11:17-23
"If some of the branches were broken off, and you, although a wild olive shoot, were grafted in among the others and now share in the nourishing root of the olive tree, do not be arrogant toward the branches. If you are, remember it is not you who support the root, but the root that supports you. Then you will say, 'Branches were broken off so that I might be grafted in.' That is true. They were broken off because of their unbelief, but you stand fast through faith. So do not become proud, but fear. For if God did not spare the natural branches, neither will he spare you. Note then the kindness and the severity of God: severity toward those who have

fallen, but God's kindness to you, provided you continue in his kindness. Otherwise you too will be cut off. And even they, if they do not continue in their unbelief, will be grafted in, for God has the power to graft them in again."

Ever since the time of Abraham the Jews have been God's people. Their relationship with Him has been tumultuous at best but the Gospel was still made available to them first. If they believed in Jesus then they continued in God's grace. But, if they rejected him then they were removed but still given the option of coming back to Christ if they believed. The same is true for Christians. We are saved because we believe. If we reject Christ after salvation then we are cut off as well.

There are many verses if studied carefully teach conditional salvation. Some are listed below for your personal consideration.

Revelation 3:2-5, Matthew 13, Matthew 18:21-35, Matthew 24:4-5; 11-13; 23-26, Matthew 25:1-13, Luke 11:24-28, Luke 12:42-46, John 6:66-71, John 8:31-32; 51, John 15:1-10, Acts 14:21-22, Romans 6:11-23, Romans 8:12-14; 17, Galatians 6:7-9, 1 Corinthians 15:1-2, Galatians 6:7-9, Philippians 2:12-16, Colossians 1:21-23, Hebrews 3:6-19, Hebrews 5:8-9, Hebrews 10:19-39

Conclusion: Clearly, the Bible teaches conditional salvation. The problem a lot of people have is that they try to make Scripture fit their theology rather than develop their theology based on Scripture. Those who support "eternal security" overlook the clear teaching of Scripture and often use analogies or examples based on human reasoning which should never be used to contradict the Bible. Why do people cling to false teachings regarding salvation? I think that sometimes it is out of fear for a loved one who has rejected Christ but hopeful thinking or bad theology will not secure them a place in heaven. Also, I have noticed that many people believe in false teachings because they were raised that way or they have never tested their faith. Remember: Truth can stand the test. You never need to believe something simply because someone else says it is true. As a matter of fact, that can be very dangerous. Search the Scripture, test the doctrine, measure what you believe against the standard of God's word. *"These Jews were more noble than those in Thessalonica; they received the word with all eagerness, examining the Scriptures daily to see if these things were so. Many of them therefore believed..." (Acts 17:11-12)*

5. Sanctification

At times I have wondered what it would look like if people came to church looking as mature physically as they are spiritually. How many would look strong and fit and how many would look like an out of work sumo wrestler? How many would be babies nursing on bottles or sucking on a pacifier? Who would be the wimp on the beach that gets sand kicked in his face and how many would be the stars of muscle beach? *"For though by this time you ought to be teachers, you need someone to teach you again the basic principles of the oracles of God. You need milk, not solid food, for everyone who lives on milk is unskilled in the word of righteousness, since he is a child. But solid food is for the mature, for those who have their powers of discernment trained by constant practice to distinguish good from evil." (Hebrews 5:12-14)*

When we accept Christ as our Savior, God expects us to have spiritual growth until the day we die. We are to become more like Jesus and less like the devil! We are never in a neutral state. We are either growing spiritually or declining spiritually. The word "sanctification" is a theological term used to describe the process of becoming holy in thought, motive and behavior.

It may be shocking to learn but God requires all of us to be perfect! *"You therefore must be perfect, as your heavenly Father is perfect." (Matthew 5:48)* This may seem impossible but when you understand that God never requires of us something that is impossible then you need to understand what He means.

In the Bible there are two types of sin. One is simply "missing the mark" in regard to perfection. All of us in this life will never be absolutely perfect. But there is another type of sin described in the Bible and that is willfully doing what we know is wrong (sins of commission) or not doing what we know is right (sins of omission). At the time of genuine conversion our attitude about sin changes.

No longer do we want to do those things that are displeasing to God. We are still tempted but we don't want to sin.

During the early days of the Church there were individuals who believed that since God gets glory for forgiving sin then the way to give him more glory is to sin more so that He forgives more. Paul was very clear in regard to that kind of stupidity. *"What shall we say then? Are we to continue in sin that grace may abound? By no means! How can we who died to sin still live in it? (Romans 6:1-2)* The word "died" in this passage is past tense. It means that it is not normal for a Christian to sin. A normal life for a Christian is to live a grateful life of obedience to Christ and His word!

Instant holiness in regard to our behavior doesn't just happen. It isn't like we can have our "instant holiness cereal" every morning! This was something that was very frustrating for me when I was a new Christian. I wanted to serve the Lord but I had a big problem with my thought life. For years I had followed the path of immoral thinking. As an adult when I rededicated my life to the Lord I hated the thoughts I knew were displeasing to Him.

I sought out help from a mature Christian who helped me to understand that even though I was forgiven for my sins I needed to change my way of thinking by replacing sinful thoughts and attitudes with new ones that honored God. It was a process. *"Do not be conformed to this world, but be transformed by the renewal of your mind, that by testing you may discern what is the will of God, what is good and acceptable and perfect." (Romans 12:2)*

The chart below helps to illustrate the process of changing sinful habit patterns to habits of holiness.

The individual's will is king. God has given us the ability to make choices about almost everything in our lives. In theology we call this "free-will." Most importantly this means that you can choose what you will think about. When we are controlled by our sinful nature our thoughts are naturally evil and self-centered. What happens is that our thoughts affect our attitudes which affect our feelings which produce certain behaviors which lead to spiritual life or death. As we continue thinking a certain way we become conditioned to continue in that direction. Habit patterns develop to where we automatically repeat behaviors without giving it any thought. The good news is that, with God's help, we can change our sinful habit patterns into holy habit patterns.

Knowing God's Word was essential to King David in his battle with sin and it is essential for you. *"How can a young man keep his way pure? By guarding it according to your word. With my whole heart I seek you; let me not wander from your commandments! I have stored up your word in my heart, that I might not sin against you."* (Psalm 119:9-11)

The key to everything is to firmly decide to replace sinful thoughts with Biblical thoughts. This takes discipline. Spiritual fitness is not something that just happens. You have to work at it. Too many people are spiritually like the person who sits on the couch with two bags of chips and a case of soft drinks playing video games all day and wonders why he has no energy while he develops heart disease and other ailments! How can I say this kindly… Get off your back side and get to work!

Frankly, a lot of people in our culture have become lazy. Many people want something for nothing and quick and easy results. Even the microwave doesn't go fast enough. I know a man who told me that he tried to diet once. He weighed himself in the morning, starved himself all day and weighed more in the evening so he decided it wasn't worth it.

As in physical fitness, spiritual fitness requires a careful, consistent plan. It is difficult to see daily changes but over time amazing results can be achieved. The first and most crucial thing necessary is to saturate your mind with Scripture. Reading the Bible every day is not hard to do. Most people think nothing of watching a television program for an hour but put no effort into daily Bible reading. I can guarantee you that reading the Bible for an hour a day will do a lot more to enrich your life than playing video games, watching stupid sitcoms or some other mind wasting entertainment. Just try it. I'm not telling you to quit watching television but just replace one program with a study of God's word and you, along with those who know you, will be amazed at the results!

Even though personal discipline is important in the sanctification process, it isn't all up to us. Human effort by itself will fall way short but, fortunately, God is willing to help. God will grant to the fully consecrated believer the power of the Holy Spirit to enable him or her to be victorious over sin. Jesus said, *"You will receive power when the Holy Spirit has come upon you, and you will be my witnesses in Jerusalem and in all Judea and Samaria, and to the end of the earth." (Acts 1:8)*

As we constantly yield ourselves to the Holy Spirit he guides us, comforts us, teaches us and has his nature shown in our lives. *"The fruit of the Spirit is love, joy, peace, patience, kindness, goodness, faithfulness, gentleness, self-control" (Galatians 5:22-23)*

A holy life is maintained through a continual, progressive, faith in and obedience to the Lord Jesus Christ. *"If we walk in the light, as he is in the light, we have fellowship with one another, and the blood of Jesus his Son cleanses us from all sin." (1 John 1:7)* It is possible, though unlikely, to be holy one moment and a sinner the next. It all depends on your choice to follow the Lord or not. Sadly, a lot of Christians get so involved with distractions in life that they fail to be aware of God's presence on a consistent basis. An important thing to note is that if you are a Christian and you choose to sin then the Holy Spirit will convict you of that sin and offer restoration if you submit to Him.

In the 1600s there was a monk by the name of Brother Lawrence. He was assigned to the monastery kitchen where he did the tedious chores of cooking and cleaning. He was the low man on the totem pole and certainly had no earthly position of glory. And yet, he is known for his holiness and great joy in the Lord. He came to realize that true spirituality and purpose in life comes not from the things of this world but rather from a continual awareness of God's presence. He saw all of his work as an opportunity to serve the Lord. Brother Lawrence wrote, "Men invent means and methods of coming at God's love, they learn rules and set up devices to remind them of that love, and it seems like a world of trouble to bring oneself into the consciousness of God's presence. Yet it might be so simple. Is it not quicker and easier just to do our common business wholly for the love of him?"

For Brother Lawrence, "common business," no matter how simple or routine could be an expression of God's love. The sacredness or worldly status of a job mattered less than the motivation behind it. "Nor is it needful that we should have great things to do. . . We can do little things for God; I turn the cake that is frying on the pan for love of him, and that done, if there is nothing else to call me, I prostrate myself in worship before him, who has given me grace to work; afterwards I rise happier than a king. It is enough for me to pick up but a straw from the ground for the love of God."

People came from all over to seek spiritual guidance from Brother Lawrence. His thoughts, philosophy and advice eventually were written down in a book that has become a spiritual classic entitled "The Practice of the Presence of God" which I highly recommend. Interestingly enough, God has called us to be perfect!

Sanctification is expressed as perfect love; which is a perfection of motive and devotion to both God and other people. When asked what was the greatest commandment Jesus replied, *"You shall love the Lord your God with all your heart and with all your soul and with all your mind. This is the great and first commandment. And a second is like it: You shall love your neighbor as yourself. On these two commandments depend all the Law and the Prophets." (Matthew 22:37-40)*

To love others does not mean that we give them everything that they want but rather we desire, and attempt to assist in, whatever is best for the individual. At times we don't know what that is, but a good approach is to try to live by what is known as The Golden Rule: *"Whatever you wish that others would do to you, do also to them, for this is the Law and the Prophets." (Matthew 7:12)*

Section 7
Ecclesiology

Ecclesiology is the study of the nature of the Church.

The Greek word ecclesia means an assembly or body of "called out ones." Today the word church is used to describe both people and organizations: "Church" (capital C) is: All born again believers (the body of Christ); "church" (small c) is: Any religious group or local church.

1. Work of the Holy Spirit in the Church

The Holy Spirit is the one who administers the life of Christ in people making them members of His spiritual body, the Church. _"In one Spirit we were all baptized into one body—Jews or Greeks, slaves or free—and all were made to drink of one Spirit. For the body does not consist of one member but of many.(1 Corinthians 12:13-14)_ The Holy Spirit also dwells in the holy temple he made. _"Do you not know that your body is a temple of the Holy Spirit within you, whom you have from God?" (1Corinthians 6:19)_

The Church is not an independent creation of the Spirit, but an enlargement of the incarnate life of Christ. _"You are the body of Christ and individually members of it." (1 Corinthians 12:27)_

2. Major Functions of the Church

Evangelism – Helping others come to a genuine living knowledge of the Lord Jesus Christ and experience salvation from sin. _"He said to them, 'Go into all the world and proclaim the gospel to the whole creation.'" (Mark 16:15)_

Discipleship – Helping others experience sanctification by discovering and applying the deep truths of God. _"Go therefore and make disciples of all nations, baptizing them in the name of the Father and of the Son and of the Holy Spirit, teaching them to observe all that I have commanded you. And behold, I am with you always, to the end of the age. (Matthew 28:19-20)_

Ministry – Exercising Spiritual Gifts to further the work of Christ in the Church and in the world.
"Having gifts that differ according to the grace given to us, let us use them." (Romans 12:6)

Community – The Church should meet together on a regular basis for corporate worship, prayer, instruction and fellowship. *"Let us consider how to stir up one another to love and good works, not neglecting to meet together, as is the habit of some, but encouraging one another, and all the more as you see the Day drawing near." (Hebrews 10:24-25)*

3. Things to look for in a Local Church or Denomination

1. Biblical doctrine and statement of faith
A lot of people may choose a church or attend one for years and have no idea what it has as its core teachings. Whether you realize it or not, what is taught will strongly influence yourself and your family.
"Keep a close watch on yourself and on the teaching. Persist in this, for by so doing you will save both yourself and your hearers." (1 Timothy 4:16)

2. Biblical preaching
Some preachers will read one verse, close their Bible then preach a whole sermon without discussing the Scripture at all. I once attended a church in Korea that, at the time, was the largest Christian church in the world. The whole message revolved around the idea that the people deserved to have a cell phone! When looking for a church make sure that the preaching is clearly on the Bible and its application to life, not on wishful thinking or self-centered philosophy.
"I charge you in the presence of God and of Christ Jesus, who is to judge the living and the dead, and by his appearing and his kingdom: preach the word; be ready in season and out of season; reprove, rebuke, and exhort, with complete patience and teaching. For the time is coming when people will not endure sound teaching,

but having itching ears they will accumulate for themselves teachers to suit their own passions, and will turn away from listening to the truth and wander off into myths." (2 Timothy 4:1-4)

3. A sense of genuine worship

Worship of God should be a major aspect of any church. This is usually found in the music that is played or sang. For many years hymns were the standard, then newer songs, usually called choruses, began to play a significant part in many churches. This was sometimes met with great resistance even resulting in church splits! There are even some churches today that insist that "contemporary music" is evil and will only use the old hymns. Little do most of them know that when the hymns were first written they were the "contemporary music" of their day. As a matter of fact, many of the tunes of the hymns were old bar room songs with the lyrics changed to Christian themes! Church music can basically be divided into two different types: 1) Songs about God, or what he has done and 2) Songs to God for who He is or what He has done. What is important is what is going on in the heart of the person who is singing, or playing an instrument. Are they truly worshiping God, or are they simply going through the motions or, worse yet, caught up in the excitement of entertainment?

Of major concern should be the theology of the music. Many hymns and choruses teach unbiblical and even heretical theology! Many song writers have very poor or erroneous understandings of what is truly biblical theology. Often people choose "worship" music because it has a catchy tune, sounds nice or gives an emotional high. While emotions are an important part of genuine worship, they should spring from solid, biblical foundations that enforce accurate theology. Personally, I like some of the old hymns because that is the tradition I grew up with so they are sentimental, but if I really want to engage with God then the contemporary music that is directed specifically toward God leads me into a much deeper sense of worship and encounter with the Almighty.

4. A devotion to Bible Study and Prayer

The number one best selling book in the history of the world is the Bible. Yet, a responsible survey found that only 20% of Americans have read the whole Bible with only 11% reading a part of it each day. Many people will spend hours watching mindless television, or engaging in social media but devote little or no time to the greatest book ever written! Is it any wonder that the world is in the mess it is in? While most Americans don't bother to read the Bible there are still over 250,000,000 people who do not have the Scripture in their own language so they couldn't read it if they wanted to!

5. **Spiritual accountability for members & especially leadership.**

Sometimes people in authority are viewed as being perfect in their ideas, decisions and actions. A secular example would be how people believe inaccurate information from politicians, news sources or articles on the internet. It must be true if an "expert" says it is. This is also how many people view medical doctors. If the doctor makes a judgment on a person's health it must be right! Sadly, blind acceptance of doctor's diagnoses has sometimes resulted in drastic consequences including death. I think a more serious concern is how many spiritual leaders teach ideas and philosophies that lead people down a path of sin or false belief which can encourage a person to believe something is true, when it is not. That belief could cost them their financial resources, personal joy and even their eternal destiny. Another problem is when members are allowed to continue in obvious sin without being confronted by mature Christians. Tolerated sin among members is a bad witness to the world and often results in others following their example.

"It is actually reported that there is sexual immorality among you, and of a kind that is not tolerated even among pagans, for a man has his father's wife. And you are arrogant! Ought you not rather to mourn? Let him who has done this be removed from among you. For though absent in body, I am present in spirit; and as if present, I have already pronounced judgment on the one who did such a thing. When you are assembled in the name of the Lord Jesus and my spirit is present, with the power of our Lord Jesus, you are to deliver this man to Satan for the destruction of the flesh, so that his spirit may be saved in the day of the Lord. Your boasting is not good. Do you not know that a little leaven leavens the whole lump? Cleanse out the old leaven that you may be a new lump, as you really are unleavened. For Christ, our Passover lamb, has been sacrificed. Let us therefore celebrate the festival, not with the old

leaven, the leaven of malice and evil, but with the unleavened bread of sincerity and truth. I wrote to you in my letter not to associate with sexually immoral people—not at all meaning the sexually immoral of this world, or the greedy and swindlers, or idolaters, since then you would need to go out of the world. But now I am writing to you not to associate with anyone who bears the name of brother if he is guilty of sexual immorality or greed, or is an idolater, reviler, drunkard, or swindler—not even to eat with such a one. For what have I to do with judging outsiders? Is it not those inside the church whom you are to judge? God judges those outside. 'Purge the evil person from among you.'" (1 Corinthians 5:1-12)

6. **A sense of mission to carry out the work of Christ in the world.**

Some churches spend all of their resources on making those who attend feel comfortable and entertained. While church should be an enjoyable experience the main focus should be to worship God. Emphasis should also be placed on winning people to Christ and making them into devoted mature disciples. Winning others and discipling them is a specific command of Christ that is largely ignored by most Christians. Who is it that you are attempting to lead to a solid commitment to Jesus? What are you doing to advance the Kingdom of Christ? *"Jesus came and said to them, 'All authority in heaven and on earth has been given to me. Go therefore and make disciples of all nations, baptizing them in the name of the Father and of the Son and of the Holy Spirit, teaching them to observe all that I have commanded you. And behold, I am with you always, to the end of the age." (Matthew 28:18-20)*

4. Biblical model for Christian leadership

In order for any significant success in an organization there must be effective leadership. This is essential in the proper functioning of the church and other religious endeavors. In establishing and insuring the appropriate functioning of the Church and its mission, the Bible basically speaks of two different important influences: spiritual gifts of individual believers and church offices.

Not all Christian organizations will have the same names for persons in leadership but the biblical principles can apply to all. Within the church the bible gives two distinct offices of leadership: Elders and Deacons. These are leadership positions and are not spiritual gift positions. But it should be noted that certain spiritual gifts work well with different job responsibilities. (See Appendix 2 for spiritual gifts)

The Offices of Elder and Deacon

Elder
1. Above Reproach - *1 Timothy 3:2*
2. Faithful to His Wife - *1 Timothy 3:2*
3. Self-controlled - *1 Timothy 3:2; Titus 1:7*
4. Live Wisely - *1 Timothy 3:2*
5. Have a Good Reputation - *1 Timothy 3:2*
6. Be Hospitable - *1 Timothy 3:2*
7. Be Able to Teach - *1 Timothy 3:2*
8. Not be a Heavy Drinker - *1 Timothy 3:3*
9. Not Violent but Gentle - *1 Timothy 3:3; Titus 1:7*
10. Not Quarrelsome - *1 Timothy 3:3*
11. Not a Lover of Money - *1 Timothy 3:3*
12. Manage His Own Household - *1 Timothy 3:3*
13. Not a Recent Convert - *1 Timothy 3:6*
14. Have a good reputation with outsiders - *1 Timothy 3:7*
15. Not Arrogant - *Titus 1:7*
16. Not quick-tempered - *Titus 1:7*
17. Loves What is Good - *Titus 1:8*
18. Upright and Holy - *Titus 1:8*

Deacons
1. Well Respected - *1 Timothy 3:8*
2. Have Integrity - *1 Timothy 3:8*
3. Not be a Heavy Drinker - *1 Timothy 3:8*
4. Not Dishonest with Money - *1 Timothy 3:8*
5. Committed to the Gospel - *1 Timothy 3:9*
6. Have a Clear Conscience - *1 Timothy 3:8*
7. Faithful to His Wife - *1 Timothy 3:12*
8. Must manage his children and household well - *1 Timothy 3:12*

Responsibilities

Elders
1. Administrative – to rule the church - _1 Timothy 5:17; Titus 1:7_
2. Pastoral – to shepherd the church - _1 Peter 5:2; Jude 12_
3. Educational – to teach the church - _Ephesians 4:12-13; 1 Timothy 3:2_
4. Officiate – to lead in the functions of the church - _James 5:14_
5. Representative – to represent the church - _Acts 20:17; 1 Timothy 5:17_

Deacons
To help the poor and relieve the elders- _Acts 6:1-6_

5. Church Membership
You do not need to be a member of a local church to go to heaven. Membership into the Universal Church happens when you accept Christ as your Savior and turn your life over to Him. We would call that the Church with a capital C. That Church consists of all truly born again believers and is essential for salvation. In the New Testament almost all of the references to "church" were in regard to a specific group of Christians. Membership in a local church, or Christian organization, while not necessary for salvation is an important part of our Christian experience for the following reasons.
1. Membership demonstrates an individual's commitment to the mission of the Christian organization.
2. Membership strengthens the influence of the organization in the community and the world.
3. Membership demonstrates an agreement with key doctrines, traditions and practices of the group of believers.
4. Membership is often required for leadership positions and voting.
5. Membership is an act of submission to God ordained authority within the Church.
6. Membership enhances the care and protection one receives from other members.

6. Church Discipline
When I was a child I learned something very quickly. I didn't like to be disciplined! One of my least favorite verses was _"Whoever_

spares the rod hates his son, but he who loves him is diligent to discipline him." (Proverbs 13:24)

It is only after we mature that we understand the importance of discipline. We have all seen the results of a life that hasn't learned the importance of discipline. Both self-discipline and correction administered by others. Discipline enhances growth, strengthens character, saves lives and helps us mature in Christ. *"For the moment all discipline seems painful rather than pleasant, but later it yields the peaceful fruit of righteousness to those who have been trained by it." (Hebrews 12:11)*

Christian discipline is clearly biblical and is essential in the Church. Sadly in many contemporary Christian organizations discipline is almost non-existent. Tolerance and non-confrontation are the motivational philosophies of many groups. The desire to get a greater number of members causes many churches and Christian organizations to be careful not to offend anyone. What sometimes happens is that the church or organization becomes full of individuals who would call themselves Christians but are in many cases living openly in sin, which, according to the Bible means that you are not a Christian!

What often takes place is that with many churches available, if a person is confronted about their sin they simply go to a different church. I personally feel that one of the reasons why biblical Christianity and Christian values are so weak in America and many other parts of the world is because the church, starting with the pastors, have failed to follow what the Bible has to say about church discipline. For a good example of how God feels about the subject, take a look at the seven churches in the book of *Revelation*.

You might ask, "How do you confront someone living in sin?" As always, the Bible clearly tells us what to do. To begin with, you must check your own attitude: *"Do nothing from selfish ambition or conceit, but in humility count others more significant than yourselves. Let each of you look not only to his own interests, but also to the interests of others." (Philippians 2:3-4)* Once you have

71

the proper spirit and you have sought wisdom from the Lord then
apply the biblical concepts in confronting a believer who sins:

You become aware of a sin in the life of another believer

You go to that person privately and talk with them about the sin.
"If your brother sins against you, go and tell him his fault, between you and him alone. If he listens to you, you have gained your brother. (Matthew 18:15) "If your brother sins, rebuke him, and if he repents, forgive him."
Luke 17:3

If the person continues to sin

Confront the person with two or three witnesses.
"But if he does not listen, take one or two others along with you, that every charge may be established by the evidence of two or three witnesses." (Matthew 18:16) "A single witness shall not suffice against a person for any crime or for any wrong in connection with any offense that he has committed. Only on the evidence of two witnesses or of three witnesses shall a charge be established." (Deuteronomy 19:15

If the person continues to sin

Remove the person from the church & consider them as someone needing salvation.
"If he refuses to listen to them, tell it to the church. And if he refuses to listen even to the church, let him be to you as a Gentile and a tax collector. "
(Matthew 18:17) "But now I am writing to you not to associate with anyone who bears the name of brother if he is guilty of sexual immorality or greed, or is an idolater, reviler, drunkard, or swindler—not even to eat with such a one." (1 Corinthians 5:11) "I appeal to you, brothers, to watch out for those who cause divisions and create obstacles contrary to the doctrine that you have been taught; avoid them. For such persons do not serve our Lord Christ, but their own appetites, and by smooth talk and flattery they deceive the hearts of the naive." Romans 16:17-18

If the person continues to sin

Reprove the person before the church. *"If he refuses to listen to them, tell it to the church." (Matthew 18:17)* *" As for those who persist in sin, rebuke them in the presence of all, so that the rest may stand in fear." (1 Timothy 5:20)*

Confronting a person who claims to be a Christian but is living in sin is not an easy thing to do. But, consider the possible consequences if you do nothing.

They may die (spiritual, mental or physical). *"My brothers, if anyone among you wanders from the truth and someone brings him back, let him know that whoever brings back a sinner from his wandering will save his soul from death and will cover a multitude of sins." (James 5:19-20)*

"Each person is tempted when he is lured and enticed by his own desire. Then desire when it has conceived gives birth to sin, and sin when it is fully grown brings forth death." (James 1:14-15)

"If anyone sees his brother committing a sin not leading to death, he shall ask, and God will give him life—to those who commit sins that do not lead to death. There is sin that leads to death; I do not say that one should pray for that. All wrongdoing is sin, but there is sin that does not lead to death." (1 John 5:16-17)

They live a hypocritical life and hurt the witness of the Church. *"If we say we have fellowship with him while we walk in darkness, we lie and do not practice the truth." (1 John 1:6)*

God may have to punish them. *"Whoever, therefore, eats the bread or drinks the cup of the Lord in an unworthy manner will be guilty concerning the body and blood of the Lord. Let a person examine himself, then, and so eat of the bread and drink of the cup. For anyone who eats and drinks without discerning the body eats and drinks judgment on himself. That is why many of you are weak and ill, and some have died." (1 Corinthians 11:27-30)*

7. Corporate Worship

The Christian life should be lived in constant fellowship with the Lord. Worship is an individual response to God's glory and grace toward us. Corporate worship is where individuals who love the Lord gather together to collectively give Him honor and praise. Historically from the very earliest time after the Resurrection, Christians met together often and especially on the first day of the week (Sunday) to pray, study the Scriptures and sing praises. God expects that Christians consistently meet together to worship and to provide encouragement to each other. *"Let us consider how to stir up one another to love and good works, not neglecting to meet together, as is the habit of some, but encouraging one another, and all the more as you see the Day drawing near." (Hebrews 10:24-25)* The following are some things that can help worship to be more meaningful, both to the individual and to God.

1. Prepare your heart and attitude before you attend the time of worship.
Often people gather together at church after a difficult week and hope to somehow be inspired before they go home. Taking the time to draw close to the Lord, repenting of any sin and focusing on His blessings will enable you to be ready for His Spirit to bless you when you meet other Christians and enter into worship.
Endeavor to be as healthy and refreshed as possible.
No matter how inspiring the music or teachings may be, if you are sleepy or hungry it will be difficult to stay focused on what is important.
2. Be well organized and make sure you have time to not be rushed.
Plan for interruptions and unexpected events. Create a positive environment for your family. Positive and negative attitudes influence those around you. Starting late and rushing around yelling at the kids or each other puts everyone in a bad mood!
3. Focus on God and the inspiration of the music when singing.
Learn to express your praise by singing and raising your hands in honor to God. You may not be used to raising your hands and showing that kind of outward expression but try it and see if it is for you. I have found that it helps me to sense a personal connection

with the Lord. *"Lift up your hands to the holy place and bless the Lord!" (Psalm 134:2)*

8. Discipleship

One of the major responsibilities of all Christians is to bring people into a saving knowledge of the Lord Jesus Christ. But it doesn't stop there. New believers need to mature in their understanding, commitment and growth as a Christian. Primary responsibility rests on the believer but other Christians also need to help. This can be accomplished on an individual basis but is often done through various organized programs. Bible Studies, home groups, Sunday School, seminars, children and youth groups, counseling and worship services with a strong Bible based message are all helpful. Jesus said, *"Go therefore and make disciples of all nations, baptizing them in the name of the Father and of the Son and of the Holy Spirit, teaching them to observe all that I have commanded you. And behold, I am with you always, to the end of the age."' Matthew 28:19-20*

Section 8
Spiritual Beings

1. Angels

My wife used to have a collection of angels. Her collection included beautiful winged female figures with flowing gowns and soft pastel colors. Even though they were nice to look at they really did not depict the angels described in Scripture. The popular cute little baby angels sometimes portrayed are also not what the bible says angels are like. When people in the Bible saw an angel, their typical response was to fall on their faces in fear and awe, not to reach out and cuddle an adorable baby. The angels described in the Bible all appear as male "human like" beings or they are terrifying, awesome creatures of power!

Some Important Facts Regarding Angels

1. The New Testament speaks of angels more than 165 times; the Old Testament more than 100 times.

2. The angels are innumerable. *"Then I looked, and I heard around the throne and the living creatures and the elders the voice of many angels, numbering myriads of myriads and thousands of thousands..." (Revelation 5:11)* and *"A stream of fire issued and came out from before him; a thousand thousands served him, and ten thousand times ten thousand stood before him..." (Daniel 7:10)*

3. The angels were created prior to God's creation of the earth. *"Where were you when I laid the foundation of the earth? Tell me, if you have understanding. Who determined its measurements— surely you know! Or who stretched the line upon it? On what were its bases sunk, or who laid its cornerstone, when the morning stars sang together and all the sons of God shouted for joy?" (Job 38:4-7)*

4. God often uses angels as His means of answering the prayers of His people.

"While I was speaking and praying, confessing my sin and the sin of my people Israel, and presenting my plea before the Lord my God for the holy hill of my God, while I was speaking in prayer, the man Gabriel, whom I had seen in the vision at the first, came to me in swift flight at the time of the evening sacrifice. He made me understand, speaking with me and saying, 'O Daniel, I have now come out to give you insight and understanding.'" (Daniel 9:20-22) and *"And behold, a hand touched me and set me trembling on my hands and knees. And he said to me, 'O Daniel, man greatly loved, understand the words that I speak to you, and stand upright, for now I have been sent to you.' And when he had spoken this word to me, I stood up trembling. Then he said to me, 'Fear not, Daniel, for from the first day that you set your heart to understand and humbled yourself before your God, your words have been heard, and I have come because of your words. The prince of the kingdom of Persia withstood me twenty-one days, but Michael, one of the chief princes, came to help me, for I was left there with the kings of Persia, and came to make you understand what is to happen to your people in the latter days." (Daniel 10:10-12)* and *"Peter was kept in prison, but earnest prayer for him was made to God by the church. Now when Herod was about to bring him out, on that very night, Peter was sleeping between two soldiers, bound with two chains, and sentries before the door were guarding the prison. And behold, an angel of the Lord stood next to him, and a light shone in the cell. He struck Peter on the side and woke him, saying, 'Get up quickly.' And the chains fell off his hands. And the angel said to him, 'Dress yourself and put on your sandals.' And he did so. And he said to him, 'Wrap your cloak around you and follow me.' And he went out and followed him." Acts 12:6-9)*

5. You really do have a guardian angel. Ever wonder what your angel is like? I am concerned that mine will beat me up when I get to heaven for everything I have put him through! God's angels are guardians for those who are Christian. Regarding angels *"Are they not all ministering spirits sent out to serve for the sake of those who are to inherit salvation?" (Hebrews 1:14)* and *"Because you have made the Lord your dwelling place— the Most High, who is my refuge—no evil shall be allowed to befall you, no plague come near*

your tent. For he will command his angels concerning you to guard you in all your ways..." (Psalm 91:9-11).

6. No holy angel will engage in a personal relationship with a human without pointing that person to the one true God. Scripture condemns any form of angel worship. *"Let no one disqualify you, insisting on asceticism and worship of angels..." (Colossians 2:18)*

7. Under no circumstances do angels act as mediators between humans and God. Scripture tells us that the only mediator is Jesus Christ. *"There is one God, and there is one mediator between God and men, the man Christ Jesus..." (1 Timothy 2:5)*

8. Angels often serve as messengers for God. Angels told Joseph about the birth of Jesus and what he should do. *(Matthew 1-2)* Angels told the women at the tomb of Jesus that he was alive. *"Now after the Sabbath, toward the dawn of the first day of the week, Mary Magdalene and the other Mary went to see the tomb. And behold, there was a great earthquake, for an angel of the Lord descended from heaven and came and rolled back the stone and sat on it. His appearance was like lightning, and his clothing white as snow. And for fear of him the guards trembled and became like dead men. But the angel said to the women, 'Do not be afraid, for I know that you seek Jesus who was crucified. He is not here, for he has risen, as he said. Come, see the place where he lay.'" (Matthew 28:1-6)* They also gave personal messages to Philip *"Now an angel of the Lord said to Philip, 'Rise and go toward the south to the road that goes down from Jerusalem to Gaza.'" (Acts 8:26)* and Cornelius: *"At Caesarea there was a man named Cornelius, a centurion of what was known as the Italian Cohort, a devout man who feared God with all his household, gave alms generously to the people, and prayed continually to God. About the ninth hour of the day he saw clearly in a vision an angel of God come in and say to him, 'Cornelius.' And he stared at him in terror and said, 'What is it, Lord?'" (Acts 10:1-4)*

9. Angels are sometimes used to bring judgment on the wicked. *"He let loose on them his burning anger, wrath, indignation, and distress, a company of destroying angels." (Psalm 79:49)* and *"The angel of the Lord went out and struck down 185,000 in the camp of*

the Assyrians." (Isaiah 37:36) and "On an appointed day Herod put on his royal robes, took his seat upon the throne, and delivered an oration to them. And the people were shouting, 'The voice of a god, and not of a man!' Immediately an angel of the Lord struck him down, because he did not give God the glory, and he was eaten by worms and breathed his last." (Acts 12:21-23) Also notice the many references throughout the book of Revelation in the administration of God's judgments on the earth, ie. Trumpet judgments & bowls of wrath.

10. Angels escort believers into heaven at the moment of death. "The poor man died and was carried by the angels to Abraham's side." (Luke 16:22)

11. In regard to Jesus, angels proclaimed His birth (Luke 2:9-14), took care of Him after his wilderness temptations (Matthew 4:11), strengthened Him for the crucifixion (Luke 22:43), announced his return to earth (Acts 1:9-11) and worship Him (Hebrews 1:6 & Revelation).

2. Satan and demons

Important Biblical Facts Regarding Evil Spiritual Beings

1. Even though in the beginning God created all of the angels good and holy they were given a period of probation. The angels, like people, were allowed the ability to choose between following God and His ways or rejecting Him.

2. An angelic rebellion, headed by Lucifer, arose against God. Lucifer became proud of his beauty and position and wanted to ascend to be equal with God. As a result God booted him out of heaven.

3. One third of the angels followed Lucifer in his rebellion. Why they did this no one knows other than the fact that Lucifer is a masterful deceiver. "You were the signet of perfection, full of wisdom and perfect in beauty. You were in Eden, the garden of God; every precious stone was your covering, sardius, topaz, and diamond, beryl, onyx, and jasper, sapphire, emerald, and carbuncle; and crafted in gold were your settings and your

engravings. On the day that you were created they were prepared. You were an anointed guardian cherub. I placed you; you were on the holy mountain of God; in the midst of the stones of fire you walked. You were blameless in your ways from the day you were created, till unrighteousness was found in you. In the abundance of your trade you were filled with violence in your midst, and you sinned; so I cast you as a profane thing from the mountain of God..." (Ezekiel 28:12-16) and *"How you are fallen from heaven, O Day Star, son of Dawn! How you are cut down to the ground, you who laid the nations low! You said in your heart, 'I will ascend to heaven; above the stars of God I will set my throne on high; I will sit on the mount of assembly in the far reaches of the north; I will ascend above the heights of the clouds; I will make myself like the Most High.' But you are brought down to Sheol, to the far reaches of the pit." (Isaiah 14:12-15)* Those angels who rebelled became what are called demons or "unclean spirits."

4. No one knows how many fallen angels there are. There are so many that a legion, 6,000, were in possession of one person. *"'What have you to do with me, Jesus, Son of the Most High God? I adjure you by God, do not torment me.' For he was saying to him, 'Come out of the man, you unclean spirit!' And Jesus asked him, 'What is your name?' He replied, 'My name is Legion, for we are many.'" (Mark 5:8-9)*

5. Following his expulsion from heaven, Lucifer's name was changed to Satan, which means "adversary."

6. Scriptural Descriptions of satan
-Accuser of the believer. *(Revelation 12:10)*
-Our adversary. *(1 Peter 5:8)*
-A roaring lion seeking to devour Christians *(1 Peter 5:8, 9)*
-The devil *(Matthew 4:1)*
-Our enemy (*Matthew 13:39)*
-The evil one *(1 John 5:19)*
-The father of lies *(John 8:44)*
-A murderer *(John 8:44)*
-The tempter *(Matthew 4:3)*

7. Though satan and demons can do many things to believers, Christians cannot be demon possessed. A Christian can be assaulted from without (temptation and oppression), but not from within (possession). The Holy Spirit, who is God, indwells believers thereby making demon possession impossible. _"Do you not know that your body is a temple of the Holy Spirit within you?" (1 Corinthians 6:19)_

8. Demonic oppression is a very heavy negative suppression of the spirit and joy of a person. It is stronger than temptation and is usually the result of continual yielding to negative thoughts and temptations. This can be countered by earnest prayer and filling your mind with the positive truth of God's Word. _"Whatever is true, whatever is honorable, whatever is just, whatever is pure, whatever is lovely, whatever is commendable, if there is any excellence, if there is anything worthy of praise, think about these things." Philippians 4:8_

9. God has provided spiritual armor for our defense. But we must choose to put on and use this armor. _"Therefore take up the whole armor of God, that you may be able to withstand in the evil day, and having done all, to stand firm. Stand therefore, having fastened on the belt of truth, and having put on the breastplate of righteousness, and, as shoes for your feet, having put on the readiness given by the gospel of peace. In all circumstances take up the shield of faith, with which you can extinguish all the flaming darts of the evil one; and take the helmet of salvation, and the sword of the Spirit, which is the word of God." (Ephesians 6:13-17)_

10. Having a strong knowledge and understanding of the Bible is especially important for spiritual victory. Jesus used the Word of God to defeat the devil during His wilderness temptations. _(Matthew 4)_ We must do the same.

11. In spiritual things you can never be a wimp. Christians are to take a decisive stand against satan. _"Submit yourselves therefore to God. Resist the devil, and he will flee from you." (James 4:7)_ I have a friend who told me that one of the ways he resists temptation is to use temptation as an alert to pray for someone. For example, in the area of lust it is difficult to think wrong thoughts

when you are praying for that other person! Also, if every time you are tempted you pray, then you can be sure that satan and his cohorts are going to back away.

12. A lot of people are intrigued with the dark side of things but Christians should have nothing to do with the occult. Involvement in occult activities gives the devil and demons opportunity to work in your life. I once knew a teenage girl who had recently accepted Christ but strange things were happening in her house. Suddenly doors would slam when there was no breeze. She would be in her room and a deep spiritual foreboding would often come over her. The toilet would even flush on its own! She asked me for help because it was freaking her out, to say the least! When I visited her I discovered a large box of horoscopes and occult items under her bed. When we destroyed them and prayed for the Lord to remove any evil presence from her house all of the strange things stopped. *"There shall not be found among you anyone who burns his son or his daughter as an offering, anyone who practices divination or tells fortunes or interprets omens, or a sorcerer or a charmer or a medium or a necromancer or one who inquires of the dead, for whoever does these things is an abomination to the Lord. And because of these abominations the Lord your God is driving them out before you. You shall be blameless before the Lord your God, for these nations, which you are about to dispossess, listen to fortune-tellers and to diviners. But as for you, the Lord your God has not allowed you to do this." (Deuteronomy 18:10-14)*

13. satan and his followers will not be a problem forever. Their fate is worse than you could ever imagine. When God brings final judgment on the world, satan and his demons will be locked away in the lake of fire for eternity. *"The devil who had deceived them was thrown into the lake of fire and sulfur where the beast and the false prophet were, and they will be tormented day and night forever and ever." (Revelation 20:10)*

Section 9
Eschatology

The various teachings concerning events that will occur at death and the end of world history is called eschatology. There are many different interpretations of what the Bible teaches regarding the end times. Some churches are dogmatic on what they believe while others are not. Even though healthy discussion can help to refine beliefs, the important point to remember is not to argue about things that are not clearly defined in Scripture. Remember that God is in control and we can trust Him. We should live our lives in such a way that we are ready for the end at any time since our personal death could occur at any moment!

In 1970 Hal Lindsey wrote a book entitled "The Late Great Planet Earth." In the book Lindsey presented the argument that the generation that was born when Israel became a nation in 1948 would not pass away until the world ended. His book was an instant national bestseller and many people came to know the Lord and become interested in prophecy. Whether or not his views come to pass is yet to be seen.

Four Views Regarding The End Times

1. Historic Premillennialism
1. The return of Christ will be preceded by certain signs, then followed by a period of peace and righteousness in which Christ will reign on earth in person as King.

2. The Rapture and the Second Coming are simultaneous; Christ returns to reign on earth.

3. The Millennium is both present and future. Christ is now reigning in heaven. The Millennium is not necessarily 1,000 years.

4. There will be a Judgment and separation at the Second Coming. The final Great White Throne Judgment will be at the end of the Tribulation.

5. The Church will go through the future Tribulation.

6. There is some distinction between Israel and the Church. There is a future for Israel, but the Church is the spiritual Israel.

7. The dominant eschatological interpretation in the first three centuries of the Christian church. (Early church fathers: Irenaeus, Justin Martyr, Tertullian)

2. Dispensational Premillennialism

1. The Second Coming is in two phases. First, the rapture of the Church. Second, Jesus will come to the earth 7 years later after the Great Tribulation.

2. There is a distinction in judgment:
>   1. Believers' works will be judged at the time of the rapture.
>   2. Jews and Gentiles will be judged at the end of the Tribulation.
>   3. Unbelievers will be judged at the end of the Millennium.

3. There will be a resurrection of believers at the beginning of the Millennium. A resurrection of unbelievers will be at the end of the Millennium.

4. At the Second Coming Christ inaugurates a literal 1,000 year Millennium on earth.

5. There are different views regarding the Rapture. The pre-tribulation view is that the church is raptured prior to the Great Tribulation. Some teach that the Rapture is in the middle of a literal seven years of tribulation. Others teach that it is at the end.

6. There is a complete distinction between Israel and the Church. There is a distinct program for each.

7. This view developed during the 1800's and is now the popular view among protestant Christians in the United States. (C.E. Scofield, Hal Lindsey, Chuck Missler)

3. Postmillennialism

1. The kingdom of God is now extended through teaching, preaching, evangelism and missionary activities.

2. The world is to be Christianized, and the result will be a long period of peace and prosperity called the Millennium. This will be followed by Christ's return.

3. The return of Christ is a single event. There is no distinction between the Rapture and Second Coming; Christ returns after the millennium.

4. The Church is the new Israel. There is no distinction between Israel and the Church.

5. There is a general resurrection and judgment of believers and unbelievers at second coming of Christ.

6. Tribulation is experienced in this present age.

7. The present age blends into the Millennium because of the progress of the Gospel.

8. Popular through-out periods of time in Church History. Gaining popularity today. (Augustine, John Wesley combined Historical Premillennialism with Postmillennialism)

4. Amillennialism

1. The Bible teaches a continuous parallel growth of good and evil in the world between the first and second coming of Christ.

2. The kingdom of God is now present in the world through His Word, His Spirit, His Church.

3. There is no literal Millennium on earth after the second coming. The kingdom is already present in the Church Age.

4. The second coming of Christ is a single event with no distinction between the rapture and the second coming. This event introduces the eternal state.

5. The general resurrection of believers and unbelievers is at the second coming of Christ.

6. There is a general judgment of all people.

7. Tribulation is experienced in this present age.

8. The Church is the new Israel. There is no distinction between Israel and the Church.

9. Reformed theologians and the Roman Catholic Church believe this view.

Section 10
Suffering - Physical Death - Heaven & Hell

Suffering and death came into the world as a result of the Fall. *(Genesis 3)*

1. Why we Suffer

1. Natural Consequences of living in a fallen world. *(Genesis 3)*

2. To learn God's laws. *"It is good for me that I was afflicted, that I might learn your statutes." (Psalm 119:71)*

3. To discipline or punish the person who sins. *"'The Lord disciplines the one he loves, and chastises every son whom he receives.' It is for discipline that you have to endure. God is treating you as sons. For what son is there whom his father does not discipline?" (Hebrews 12:6-7)*

4. To prepare us for a coming glory. *"Beloved, do not be surprised at the fiery trial when it comes upon you to test you, as though something strange were happening to you. But rejoice insofar as you share Christ's sufferings, that you may also rejoice and be glad when his glory is revealed." (1 Peter 4:12,13)*

5. To help us grow spiritually. *"Count it all joy, my brothers, when you meet trials of various kinds, for you know that the testing of your faith produces steadfastness. And let steadfastness have its full effect, that you may be perfect and complete, lacking in nothing." (James 1:2-4)*

6. To help us to witness. *"Blessed be the God and Father of our Lord Jesus Christ, the Father of mercies and God of all comfort, who comforts us in all our affliction, so that we may be able to comfort those who are in any affliction, with the comfort with which we ourselves are comforted by God." (2 Corinthians 1:3-4)*

2. Physical Death

1. Physical death came upon the earth because of the Fall.
"Of the tree of the knowledge of good and evil you shall not eat, for in the day that you eat of it you shall surely die." (Genesis 2:17) and
"Sin came into the world through one man, and death through sin,

and so death spread to all men because all sinned." (Romans 5:12) and "For as by a man came death, by a man has come also the resurrection of the dead. For as in Adam all die, so also in Christ shall all be made alive." (1 Corinthians 15:21-22)

2. Physical death is the separation of the spirit from the body. When a person dies they enter into the presence of God. They do not wait in a state of "soul sleep." "We are of good courage, and we would rather be away from the body and at home with the Lord." (2 Corinthians 5:8)

3. Christ, through His death on the cross, broke the power of the devil. "Since therefore the children share in flesh and blood, he himself likewise partook of the same things, that through death he might destroy the one who has the power of death, that is, the devil, and deliver all those who through fear of death were subject to lifelong slavery." (Hebrews 2:14-15)

4. For Christians, God provides grace at the time of death to help in the transition to heaven. (Psalm 23)

5. At the end of time our earthly bodies will be resurrected to become spiritual bodies perfect in every way.
"So is it with the resurrection of the dead. What is sown is perishable; what is raised is imperishable. It is sown in dishonor; it is raised in glory. It is sown in weakness; it is raised in power. It is sown a natural body; it is raised a spiritual body. If there is a natural body, there is also a spiritual body... For this perishable body must put on the imperishable, and this mortal body must put on immortality." (1 Corinthians 15:43-44; 53)

3. Hell

1. Description of Eternal Punishment
1. Darkness with weeping and gnashing of teeth - "The outer darkness. In that place there will be weeping and gnashing of teeth." (Matthew 8:12)
2. Furnace of fire - "So it will be at the end of the age. The angels will come out and separate the evil from the righteous and throw them into the fiery furnace. In that place there will be weeping and gnashing of teeth." (Matthew 13:49-50)

3. Eternal fire - *"Then he will say to those on his left, 'Depart from me, you cursed, into the eternal fire prepared for the devil and his angels." (Matthew 25:41)*

4. Unquenchable fire - *"His winnowing fork is in his hand, to clear his threshing floor and to gather the wheat into his barn, but the chaff he will burn with unquenchable fire." (Luke 3:17)*

5. Bottomless pit - *"And the fifth angel blew his trumpet, and I saw a star fallen from heaven to earth, and he was given the key to the shaft of the bottomless pit. He opened the shaft of the bottomless pit, and from the shaft rose smoke like the smoke of a great furnace, and the sun and the air were darkened with the smoke from the shaft. Then from the smoke came locusts on the earth, and they were given power like the power of scorpions of the earth. They were told not to harm the grass of the earth or any green plant or any tree, but only those people who do not have the seal of God on their foreheads. They were allowed to torment them for five months, but not to kill them, and their torment was like the torment of a scorpion when it stings someone. And in those days people will seek death and will not find it. They will long to die, but death will flee from them. In appearance the locusts were like horses prepared for battle: on their heads were what looked like crowns of gold; their faces were like human faces, their hair like women's hair, and their teeth like lions' teeth; they had breastplates like breastplates of iron, and the noise of their wings was like the noise of many chariots with horses rushing into battle. They have tails and stings like scorpions, and their power to hurt people for five months is in their tails. They have as king over them the angel of the bottomless pit. His name in Hebrew is Abaddon, and in Greek he is called Apollyon." (Revelation 9:1-11)*

6. Torment forever, no rest day or night - *"If anyone worships the beast and its image and receives a mark on his forehead or on his hand, he also will drink the wine of God's wrath, poured full strength into the cup of his anger, and he will be tormented with fire and sulfur in the presence of the holy angels and in the presence of the Lamb. And the smoke of their torment goes up forever and ever, and they have no rest, day or night, these worshipers of the beast and its image, and whoever receives the mark of its name." (Revelation 14:10-11)*

7. Lake of fire - *"The cowardly, the faithless, the detestable, as for murderers, the sexually immoral, sorcerers, idolaters, and all liars, their portion will be in the lake that burns with fire and sulfur, which is the second death." (Revelation 21:8)*

2. Participants in Eternal Punishment
1. Satan - *"The devil who had deceived them was thrown into the lake of fire and sulfur where the beast and the false prophet were, and they will be tormented day and night forever and ever." (Revelation 20:10)*
2. The beast and the false prophet - *"The devil who had deceived them was thrown into the lake of fire and sulfur where the beast and the false prophet were, and they will be tormented day and night forever and ever." (Revelation 20:10)*
3. Evil angels - *"God did not spare angels when they sinned, but cast them into hell and committed them to chains of gloomy darkness to be kept until the judgment..." (2 Peter 2:4)*
4. Non-Christian Humans (body and soul) are cast into everlasting punishment - *"If your right hand causes you to sin, cut it off and throw it away. For it is better that you lose one of your members than that your whole body go into hell." (Matthew 5:30)* and *"Do not fear those who kill the body but cannot kill the soul. Rather fear him who can destroy both soul and body in hell. (Matthew 10:28)* and *"If anyone's name was not found written in the book of life, he was thrown into the lake of fire." (Revelation 20:15)*

3. Effects of Eternal Punishment
1. Separation from God and his glory
"When the Lord Jesus is revealed from heaven with his mighty angels in flaming fire, inflicting vengeance on those who do not know God and on those who do not obey the gospel of our Lord Jesus. They will suffer the punishment of eternal destruction, away from the presence of the Lord and from the glory of his might, when he comes on that day to be glorified in his saints, and to be marveled at among all who have believed..." (2 Thessalonians 1:9)
2. Different degrees of punishment
"That servant who knew his master's will but did not get ready or act according to his will, will receive a severe beating. But the one who did not know, and did what deserved a beating, will receive a

light beating. Everyone to whom much was given, of him much will be required, and from him to whom they entrusted much, they will demand the more." (Luke 12:47-48)

3. Final eternal state/no second chance

"'Depart from me, you cursed, into the eternal fire prepared for the devil and his angels. For I was hungry and you gave me no food, I was thirsty and you gave me no drink, I was a stranger and you did not welcome me, naked and you did not clothe me, sick and in prison and you did not visit me.' Then they also will answer, saying, 'Lord, when did we see you hungry or thirsty or a stranger or naked or sick or in prison, and did not minister to you?' Then he will answer them, saying, 'Truly, I say to you, as you did not do it to one of the least of these, you did not do it to me.' And these will go away into eternal punishment, but the righteous into eternal life." (Matthew 25:42-46)

4. Heaven
1. Description of Heaven
1. Greater than we can imagine. *"No eye has seen, nor ear heard, nor the heart of man imagined, what God has prepared for those who love him." (1 Corinthians 2:9)*

2. No evil of any kind. *"No longer will there be anything accursed, but the throne of God and of the Lamb will be in it, and his servants will worship him." (Revelation 22:3)*

3. Beautiful beyond description. *"The wall was built of jasper, while the city was pure gold, like clear glass. The foundations of the wall of the city were adorned with every kind of jewel. The first was jasper, the second sapphire, the third agate, the fourth emerald, the fifth onyx, the sixth carnelian, the seventh chrysolite, the eighth beryl, the ninth topaz, the tenth chrysoprase, the eleventh jacinth, the twelfth amethyst. And the twelve gates were twelve pearls, each of the gates made of a single pearl, and the street of the city was pure gold, like transparent glass. And I saw no temple in the city, for its temple is the Lord God the Almighty and the Lamb. And the city has no need of sun or moon to shine on it, for the glory of God gives it light, and its lamp is the Lamb. By its light will the nations walk, and the kings of the earth will bring their glory into it, and its gates will never be shut by day—and there will be no night*

there. They will bring into it the glory and the honor of the nations. But nothing unclean will ever enter it, nor anyone who does what is detestable or false, but only those who are written in the Lamb's book of life." (Revelation 21:18-27)

2. Participants in Heaven

1. Only those whose names are written in the Lamb's book of life.
"Only those who are written in the Lamb's book of life." (Revelation 21:27)

2. "born again" Christians
"Jesus answered him, 'Truly, truly, I say to you, unless one is born again he cannot see the kingdom of God.'" (John 3:3)

3. Those from Old Testament times whom God declared as righteous through the blood of Christ. *(Hebrews 11)*

4. Those who have not heard the Gospel but are judged righteous through the blood of Christ by the light they have received. This is not an established orthodox doctrine. Rather, some believe that the principles of God's justice suggest this view.
"His invisible attributes, namely, his eternal power and divine nature, have been clearly perceived, ever since the creation of the world, in the things that have been made. So they are without excuse." (Romans 1:19-20) and *"The times of ignorance God overlooked, but now he commands all people everywhere to repent, because he has fixed a day on which he will judge the world in righteousness." (Acts 17:30-31)*

3. Effects of Heaven

1. We will have perfect understanding of God and his ways. All of our "why" questions will be answered.
"Beloved, we are God's children now, and what we will be has not yet appeared; but we know that when he appears we shall be like him, because we shall see him as he is." (1 John 3:2) and *"Now we see in a mirror dimly, but then face to face. Now I know in part; then I shall know fully, even as I have been fully known." (1 Corinthians 13:12)*

2. No suffering, pain or sorrow.
"Behold, the dwelling place of God is with man. He will dwell with them, and they will be his people, and God himself will be with them as their God. He will wipe away every tear from their eyes, and death shall be no more, neither shall there be mourning, nor crying, nor pain anymore, for the former things have passed away." _(Revelation 21:3-5)_

3. Eternal life. No more struggle with sin or probationary period.
"And these (unbelievers) will go away into eternal punishment, but the righteous into eternal life."(Matthew 25:46)

Appendix 1

Why Eternal Security Is Not a Biblical Doctrine
Originally written by Philip A. Matthews. Revised and edited, with permission, by Chaplain Steven A. Wilson, PhD

Eternal Security is the doctrine that simply states, "Once saved, always saved." This doctrine teaches that once a person has been born again by trusting in Jesus as his personal Savior he can never be eternally lost after his life has ended, no matter how far that person may backslide or live and die in unconfessed sin after his initial belief in Christ. Eternal security claims that one act of faith in Christ at some time in a person's life guarantees heaven for them forevermore. According to this doctrine, there is no way for a saved person to backslide and be lost. There is no way for you to "lose your salvation." This is known in Calvinism as the "preservation of the saints."

God's Promises Are Almost Always Conditional
In commenting on this doctrine, it should first be noted that the promises of God are almost always conditional. That is, God's promised benefits are given to people as they meet the conditions stated or implied within that promise. He does not make blanket promises that apply to everybody in every place for every time except for universal promises like never destroying the earth again by flood. Most of His promises are for specific people who meet specific conditions and qualifications for the specific benefits promised.

Take _John 3:16_ for example. The promise is that _"For God so loved the world, that he gave his only Son, that whoever believes in him should not perish but have eternal life."_ There is a condition here that must be met before you can receive everlasting life: you must first believe in Jesus. If (which specifies a condition) you believe in Him, then you will not perish and you will have everlasting life. But if you do not believe in Him, then you will not have everlasting life and you will perish.

Let's take another example, _Galatians 6:9: "Let us not grow weary of doing good, for in due season we will reap, if we do not give up."_

The condition that must be met, before the promise to reap can be fulfilled, is that we must not faint. So if we faint, then it follows that we shall not reap.

But it also follows that if we have reaped, then it must be true that we did not faint. Otherwise, if we reaped and yet we did faint, then it must be true that we will reap whether we faint or not. This makes the conditional statement absolutely useless and the verse nonsensical: we shall reap if do not faint and we shall reap if we do faint. No matter what we do, we shall reap. But if this be the case, then Paul's warning against fainting is meaningless and utter nonsense. Why encourage people not to faint when in actuality it does not matter if they do or they don't?

But what is the point here? The point is that, every conditional statement in the Bible "implied or direct" is what is called a "tautology." That is, it is true both ways, forward and backward. Thus, it is true that if we do not give up, then we shall reap. And it is also true that if we do give up, then we will not reap. It is also true that if we have reaped, then we must not have given up, as well as, if we did not reap, then we must have given up. In logic, these statements condense into this: "We shall reap if and only if we do not give up. "

The Bible Is Logically Valid
Thus, the conditional, if-then-type statements of the Bible are tautological. If they are not, then many contradictions, untruths, and nonsensical statements result. This principle of logic must be used throughout the New Testament regarding all conditional statements and promises. The "If" always means "If and Only If." If it does not, then the conditional statement becomes unconditional, thus stripping the statement of all sense and meaning.

Let's take one more example, one much more directly applicable to the issue at hand, eternal security. *Second Peter 1:10-11* reads: *"Therefore, brothers, be all the more diligent to confirm your calling and election, for if you practice these qualities you will never fall. For in this way there will be richly provided for you an entrance into the eternal kingdom of our Lord and Savior Jesus Christ."* Exactly what things is Peter telling them to do? Obviously, he means the things he listed in verses 5 through 9: *"Make every effort to supplement your faith with virtue, and virtue with knowledge, and knowledge with self-control, and self-control with steadfastness, and steadfastness with godliness, and godliness with brotherly affection, and brotherly affection with love. For if these qualities are yours and are increasing, they keep you from being ineffective or unfruitful in the knowledge of our Lord Jesus Christ. For whoever lacks these qualities is so nearsighted that he is blind, having forgotten that he was cleansed from his former sins."* These are the "qualities" they are to add. In verse 9, he warns that if you lack these qualities, you are blind, cannot see afar off, and have forgotten that you were cleansed from your sins." Finally in verse 10, he says that *"Be all the more diligent to confirm your calling and election, for if you practice these qualities you will never fall."*

Now this "if" is an "if and only if." The promise is that you will never fall and you will receive a rich welcome if and only if you do these things. This rules out the possibility that you will never fall and you will receive a rich welcome without doing "these qualities." It must be true that if you do not do these things, then you will fall. If you do not do these things, then you will not receive a rich welcome. If it were possible for them to not do these things and still receive a rich welcome, then it makes no sense to warn them about it at all.

Applied to eternal security, this principle thus completely rules out the possibility of somebody getting saved, then going back out into sin and failing to do "these qualities", but still they never fall and still they will receive "entrance into the eternal kingdom." Anybody who gets saved, then fails to grow in grace, instead choosing to revert back to his old sinful lifestyle, has definitely fallen and will not be welcomed into heaven. If they make it to heaven anyway, living their sinful unrepentant lifestyle, then *2 Peter 1:10-11* and most of the rest of the New Testament" contradicts itself!

There are many other such Scriptures to which this principle of "if and only if" applies. *Revelation 2:10* promises, *"Be faithful until death, and I will give you the crown of life."* This clearly means, the Lord will give you a crown of life if and only if you are faithful until death. If you are not faithful until death, if you quit believing, if you quit doing the Lord's will, quit obeying and following His word, then it is obvious that He will not give you a crown of life. If you could get this crown of life without being faithful until death, then it would not make sense for Jesus to hold this out as some kind of reward for faithfulness and good behavior.

In *Revelation 3:1-5*, Jesus speaks of some Christians and a church that has been spiritually alive (saved) but are *"about to die."* He states why: *"I have not found your works complete in the sight of My God."* However, He finds that a few Christians there have not *"soiled their garments,"* i.e., do not have sin in their lives. These He promises will *"will walk with me in white, for they are worthy."* Then He promises: *"The one who conquers* (maintains their deeds and lives of holiness) *will be clothed thus in white garments, and I will never blot his name out of the book of life. I will confess his name before my Father and before his angels."* So He promises to do three things, dress them in white, not blot out their names, and acknowledge them before God. He will do this if and only if they will overcome. What if they do not overcome? Then it logically follows that He will not dress them in white, He will blot out their names from the book of life, and He will not acknowledge knowing them before His Father. The promise is to overcomers only. What could be more plain and logical?

There is one more of these conditional statements found in *Hebrews 3:14 "For we have come to share in Christ, if indeed we hold our original confidence firm to the end."* In other words, we are partakers in Christ if and only if we hold firmly till the end the confidence we had at first. Obviously, if we do not hold that first confidence, we will not be partakers in Christ. The promise is not just to everybody, but only to those who hold to their first confidence. The Biblical author was writing to some Christians that were being sorely tested and persecuted, and were tempted to give up. Those who let go of their faith in Christ would lose their participation and fellowship with Him. This concept was repeated in chapter *10:32-39*. He warned those Christians not to be *"...of those who shrink back and are destroyed, but of those who have faith and preserve their souls."*

The So-called Historical and "Scriptural Basis" For Eternal Security

The doctrine of eternal security is generally attributed to John Calvin, whose followers are called Calvinists or members of the Reformed tradition. But even Calvinists acknowledge that much of their doctrine originates with St. Augustine of Hippo (Algeria in Northern Africa), the Catholic (or pre-Catholic) theologian of the 4th century (354-430). He did quite a bit of writing on "Original Sin", which the reformers, Martin Luther and John Calvin, both borrowed. Calvin systematized his beliefs in the <u>Institutes of Religion</u>, a rather large work that serves as the basis for what is now known as Calvinism. His teachings regarding salvation can be summarized with the following famous acronym representing the five points of Calvinism, **TULIP**:

T = Total Depravity asserts that as a consequence of the fall of man into sin, every person is enslaved to sin. People are not by nature inclined to love God but rather to serve their own interests and to reject the rule of God. Thus, all people by their own faculties are morally unable to choose to follow God and be saved because they are unwilling to do so out of the necessity of their own natures. This eliminates freewill.

U = Unlimited Election asserts that God has chosen from eternity those whom he will bring to himself, not based on foreseen virtue, merit, or faith in those people. Instead, his choice is unconditionally grounded in his will alone. God sovereignly extends mercy to those he has chosen and to withhold mercy from those not chosen.

L = Limited Atonement asserts that Jesus' atonement was definite and certain in its purpose and in what it accomplished. This implies that only the sins of the elect were atoned for by Jesus' death. Calvinists do not believe, however, that the atonement is limited in its value or power, but rather that the atonement is limited in the sense that it is intended for some and not all.

I = Irresistible Grace asserts that the saving grace of God is effectually applied to those whom he has determined to save (that is, the elect) and overcomes their resistance to obeying the call of the gospel, bringing them to a saving faith. This means that when God sovereignly purposes to save someone, that individual certainly will be saved.

P = Perseverance of the Saints asserts that since God is sovereign and His will cannot be frustrated by humans or anything else, those whom God has called into communion with Himself will continue in faith until the end. Those who apparently fall away either never had true faith to begin with or will return to the faith. This is the point known today as "Once Saved, Always Saved." They can never be lost.

Comparison among Protestants

Topic	Calvinism	Arminianism
Human will	Total Depravity without free will permanently due to divine sovereignty	Depravity does not prevent free will
Election	Unconditional election to salvation with those outside the elect foreordained to damnation (double-predestination)	Conditional election in view of foreseen faith or unbelief
Justification	Justification is limited to those predestined to salvation, completed at Christ's death	Justification made possible for all through Christ's death, but only completed upon choosing faith in Jesus
Conversion	Irresistible call of the Holy Spirit	Resistible due to the common grace of free will
Preservation and apostasy	Perseverance of the saints: the eternally elect in Christ will necessarily persevere in faith	Preservation is conditional upon continued faith in Christ; with the possibility of a final apostasy.

These doctrines have been argued among Protestants for several centuries. Presently there are Christians who call themselves 3-point, 4-point, and 5-point Calvinists. Some denominations (e.g., many Baptists) could be classified as 1-point Calvinists, simply because they usually reject all of the first four points and hold only to Point Five, the "Perseverance of the Saints, i.e., once saved, always saved." But many major Calvinist teachers point out that Point Five is impossible without the other four points. They all stand or fall together.

The Surefire Proof That We Have Freewill

It should be obvious that most of the above differences hinge on the issue of freewill and the ability to choose morally. A great inconsistency arises when people want to believe in freewill, but then try to believe in eternal security also. The result then is that freewill allows a person to choose to believe in Christ and thereby be saved, but later choose not to believe in Christ but retain his salvation. And yet, by biblical definition, only a believer in Christ is saved. There simply is no salvation for those who do not believe in Christ. Salvation for unbelievers would contradict everything in the New Testament!

So how do we prove freewill? This is a surefire method: First of all, it is obvious that in the Garden of Eden. God gave humans the power and freewill to make a choice: To eat or not eat the fruit. Even Calvinism must admit this existence of freewill at the beginning.

Adam and Eve chose to eat of the fruit, fell into sin, became depraved, etc. Now Calvinism says that this depravity was so total and complete that, since that time, all people by their own faculties are morally unable to choose to follow God and be saved because they are unwilling to do so out of the necessity of their own natures. That is, even if we still had freewill, that depraved freewill can by necessity choose only to go a downward way, an evil path, etc., and is completely unable to choose God.

However, that is preposterous because thousands of years later, God Himself again gives the Israelites a chance to make a choice for Him and His way: _"See, I have set before you today life and good, death and evil. If you obey the commandments of the Lord your God that I command you today, by loving the Lord your God, by walking in his ways, and by keeping his commandments and his statutes and his rules, then you shall live and multiply, and the Lord your God will bless you in the land that you are entering to take possession of it. But if your heart turns away, and you will not hear, but are drawn away to worship other gods and serve them, I declare to you today, that you shall surely perish. You shall not live long in the land that you are going over the Jordan to enter and possess. I call heaven and earth to witness against you today, that I have set before you life and death, blessing and curse. Therefore choose life, that you and your offspring may live, loving the Lord your God, obeying his voice and holding fast to him, for he is your life and length of days, that you may dwell in the land that the Lord_ *swore to your fathers, to Abraham, to Isaac, and to Jacob, to give them." (Deuteronomy 30:15-20)*.

It's pretty obvious here that the Lord God of heaven believes that these people actually are able to choose Him and His way. Otherwise, if their ability to choose God and righteousness was so impaired and "totally depraved," God would be grossly unfair and utterly mean-spirited to give them a "choice" that they could not possibly make! He would be unrealistically expecting them to do something they couldn't, then judging and punishing them for failing to do something they could not possibly do! There are many other instances in the Bible where God gives fallen people a chance to exercise their freewill and expects them to choose Him. We have a choice, and because of this, the whole first foundational assumption of Calvinism, i.e., the "T in the TULIP, comes crashing down! And the rest of the theory falls with it.

The Faithfulness and Immutability of God
Most people today who believe in "once saved, always saved," don't even bother with the historical origins of eternal security, but generally base their beliefs on a few main popular arguments: (1) The faithfulness and immutability of God in His promises and gifts; (2) The analogy that spiritual birth and sonship is like natural birth and sonship; (3) The "No one can pluck them out of His hand" concept in *John 10:27-30*; and (4) The "saved by grace," not by works argument.

Regarding the faithfulness and immutability of God, it is sometimes stated by proponents that God will never take His gifts back. *"The gifts and the calling of God are irrevocable." (Romans 11:29)*. Since the gift of God is eternal life *(Romans 6:23)*, once He has given a soul eternal life, He will never take it back. They have that eternal life forever, no matter how they have behaved since they received it.

This may sound somewhat reasonable, until we read the rest of the passage and context, and discover that, once again, this promise is conditional. *Romans 6:22-23* reads: *"But now that you have been set free from sin and have become slaves of God, the fruit you get leads to sanctification and its end, eternal life. For the wages of sin*

101

is death, but the free gift of God is eternal life in Christ Jesus our Lord." The conditions to be met here are plainly stated in verse 22: *"...you have been set free from sin and have become slaves of God."* The result is eternal life. If you are not set free from sin, but have gone back into daily, habitual sin, and you are no longer a slave to God but are instead a slave again to evil, then it is not possible for the result still to be eternal life. If you go back to living in sin, then the first part of verse 23 applies to you: *"the wages of sin is death."*

God's promises are immutable, but only to those who meet the conditions. Where the conditions are not met, the performance of the promise simply does not occur. The conditions God requires always involve His holy standards. If He were to fulfill His promise regardless of whether the conditions have been met or not, He would end up having to reward something that falls far below His standards. This would force Him into actually violating His own holy nature, and God cannot and will not contradict Himself. Therefore, all conditions must be met before His promises take effect.

The Analogy of Spiritual Birth and Sonship

The concept that once a child is born into a family it is always a member of that family is another linchpin doctrine of eternal security. We can only be naturally born into this world once; we can only be born again into God's kingdom once. Once a person is born again as a child of God, they are in His family forever. Being a bad child, even a disgraceful child, does not remove them from the family. So the reasoning goes.

This would not at first appear to be faulty reasoning. But all spiritual reasoning needs some kind of validation or confirmation from Scripture, and there are no verses to support such reasoning. Who said that the spiritual family is in this respect like the natural family? Indeed, they are very different. In the natural family, babies are born into it without any choice of their wills. But no one is born into the spiritual family without making a deliberate choice to receive Christ. Our will enters the equation in the spiritual birth. Therefore, it follows that our wills must play a part in whether we remain part of the spiritual family.

We do not enter the spiritual family against our will, nor do we remain a member of the spiritual family against our will. In the New Testament, we have a few examples of men who did not choose to remain a part of the spiritual family, and Scripture records they lost out with God: Judas *"Not one of them has been lost except the son of destruction." (John 17:12)* Evidently, Judas had once been found or saved: One cannot lose something that was never possessed; (see also *Acts 1:15-26*). Another example is Hymenaeus, Philetus, and Alexander *"Some have made shipwreck of their faith, among whom are Hymenaeus and Alexander." (1 Timothy 1:19-20) "Among them are Hymenaeus and Philetus, who have swerved from the truth..." (2 Timothy 2:17-18)* They obviously had at one time possessed true faith but willfully turned away and even blasphemed the Gospel.

"No Man Can Snatch Them Out of My Hand "
This verse,, is probably the most quoted Scripture used to support eternal security. *"My sheep hear my voice, and I know them, and they follow me. I give them eternal life, and they will never perish, and no one will snatch them out of my hand. My Father, who has given them to me, is greater than all, and no one is able to snatch them out of the Father's hand." (John 10:27-29)*

Now this verse is indeed a very comforting and assuring verse from which all Christians can gather strength. However, it does not teach eternal security because, once again, this promise, too, is conditional. First of all, Jesus is talking about His sheep. His sheep have several characteristics that constitute the conditions required for this promise. In verse 27 He says that *"My sheep hear My voice, and I know them, and they follow Me."* Then He promises them eternal life. So the condition is to be one of His sheep, which means that you hear His voice. Inherent in this word "hear" is the concept of "listening , heeding and obeying." Also, He says, *"I know them."* That is, Jesus and His sheep are in fellowship and communion together; they share in the same Spirit. Sin breaks fellowship *(1 John 1; 2 Corinthians 6:14)*, and iniquity and doing one's own thing causes Jesus to say, *"I don't know you." (Matthew 25:12)*. Last, He says, *"They follow Me."* In other words, they are My disciples. They imitate Me; they obey Me. They do what I do, and go where I go. Following Jesus means that they have "denied themselves and taken up their crosses." *"If anyone would come after me, let him deny himself and take up his cross and follow me." (Matthew 16:24)*

This, by definition, is a sheep of Jesus Christ. And this is who He promises cannot be "snatched out of His hand." But this promise does not apply to some ex-Christian who has turned from following Jesus and is not hearing or obeying His voice any longer. Such a person is no longer even in the hands of the Lord! Nobody "snatched him out"; he removed himself. There is nothing stated in this verse or any other Bible passage that a person cannot voluntarily remove Himself from God's hands. We cannot lose our salvation involuntarily, but we can give it up by our own freewill.

The Saved By Grace, Not By Works Argument
Another main argument for eternal security is that which says, Since we did not receive salvation by works, we cannot be keep or maintain salvation by works. Two of the main passages to support this are: *"For by grace you have been saved through faith. And this is not your own doing; it is the gift of God, not a result of works, so that no one may boast. For we are his workmanship, created in Christ Jesus for good works, which God prepared beforehand, that we should walk in them. (Ephesians 2:8-10)* and *"He saved us, not because of works done by us in righteousness, but according to his own mercy..." (Titus 3:5)*

Verse 10 in the Ephesians passage states plainly that we are not saved by good works, but we are definitely saved for good works, i.e., to do good works. The ability to do these "good works" did not earn us our salvation but is a reliable proof or confirmation that we have salvation. Thus, it can be logically concluded that if our lives are not characterized by good works but instead by the normal habitual and sinful works of the flesh commonly committed by all unregenerate people, then we are most likely not saved. If at one time we did live a life characterized by good works but now we no longer do, then it is very likely that we once were saved but have now chosen not to be.

A passage that should prevent us from getting too dogmatic about works is *"Work out your own salvation with fear and trembling, for it is God who works in you, both to will and to work for his good pleasure." (Philippians 2:12-13)* This verse does not mean to work to earn your salvation, but to carry out the good works that help us prove or confirm our existing salvation.

General Comments on the Above Positions

One of the basic rules of biblical interpretation is that, whenever you choose to interpret a passage of Scripture one way, then that interpretation cannot possibly be true IF it contradicts other clear biblical passages. If our interpretation does contradict other clear biblical passages, then it is obvious that we need to seek for another non-contradictory interpretation. That is, if our interpretation of a certain Scripture causes conflicts with the rest of the Bible, then it must mean something other than what we thought it meant.

For example, if we decide that it is true that God only chooses certain individuals to be saved (predestination), then the biblical statement, *"The Lord is not slow to fulfill his promise as some count slowness, but is patient toward you, not wishing that any should perish, but that all should reach repentance." (2 Peter 3:9)*, is contradicted. God cannot BOTH choose only certain people to be saved but at the same time desire ALL people to be saved.

Or, if we lean too heavily on the idea that God Himself chooses or "elects " which individuals to save and those who are not chosen can never be saved (predestination again), then we eliminate the concept of freewill. When freewill is eliminated, we then contradict dozens of other Scriptures that appear to assume free-will: *"Let the one who desires take the water of life without price." (Revelation 22:17)*; *"See, I have set before you today life and good, death and evil..." (Deuteronomy 30:15)* But most of all, if we do not have free will, we cannot be held responsible and accountable. But the Scripture is plain throughout that we are accountable to God for our behavior, choices, and moral decisions.

"The queen of the South will rise up at the judgment with the men of this generation and condemn them, for she came from the ends of the earth to hear the wisdom of Solomon, and behold, something greater than Solomon is here. The men of Nineveh will rise up at the judgment with this generation and condemn it, for they

105

repented at the preaching of Jonah, and behold, something greater than Jonah is here." (Luke 11:31-32)

"Why do you pass judgment on your brother? Or you, why do you despise your brother? For we will all stand before the judgment seat of God..." (Romans 14:10)

"We must all appear before the judgment seat of Christ, so that each one may receive what is due for what he has done in the body, whether good or evil." (2 Corinthians 5:10)

"It is appointed for men to die once, and after that comes judgment..." (Hebrews 9:27)

"It is time for judgment to begin at the household of God; and if it begins with us, what will be the outcome for those who do not obey the gospel of God?" (1 Peter 4:17)

"I tell you, on the day of judgment people will give account for every careless word they speak, for by your words you will be justified, and by your words you will be condemned." (Matthew 12:36-37)

The conclusion that avoids conflicts and contradiction is that God elects all people to be saved who will call upon His name. *"If you confess with your mouth that Jesus is Lord and believe in your heart that God raised him from the dead, you will be saved. For with the heart one believes and is justified, and with the mouth one confesses and is saved. For the Scripture says, 'Everyone who believes in him will not be put to shame.' For there is no distinction between Jew and Greek; for the same Lord is Lord of all, bestowing his riches on all who call on him. For 'everyone who calls on the name of the Lord will be saved.'" (Romans 10:9-13)*

It is left up to the individual's free choice, which is talked about throughout the whole Bible, to accept or reject salvation and to accept the consequences of that choice.

Scriptures That Speak Directly of the Possibility of Backsliding
After all of the above discussion, let us now turn our attention to more direct Scriptures that contradict "once saved, always saved." What does the Bible say about backsliding and losing or forfeiting one's salvation? Is such a concept biblical or not?

Many times when discussing this issue, the idea is proposed that people do not lose their salvation; really they were never saved in the first place. Sometimes this may be true, but it is still a New Testament concept that it is possible for someone who really was saved to be lost in the end. Apostasy is a valid Bible concept, taught plainly by many Scriptures. The idea that lost souls were never saved in the first place is refuted by these Scriptures.

Below are some Scriptures that speak directly of the possibility of backsliding, i.e., of being lost after having once been saved. Remember, if we find even one instance of someone backsliding, whatever the circumstances and conditions may be, then that one instance is enough to immediately prove our point.

"It is impossible, in the case of those who have once been enlightened, who have tasted the heavenly gift, and have shared in the Holy Spirit, and have tasted the goodness of the word of God and the powers of the age to come, and then have fallen away, to restore them again to repentance, since they are crucifying once again the Son of God to their own harm and holding him up to contempt. For land that has drunk the rain that often falls on it, and produces a crop useful to those for whose sake it is cultivated, receives a blessing from God. But if it bears thorns and thistles, it is worthless and near to being cursed, and its end is to be burned." (Hebrews 6:4-8)

Obviously, whoever the Bible is speaking of is saved. If they cannot deviate from the faith, then this passage makes no sense. The terminology in this Scripture makes absolutely no sense unless there is such a thing as apostasy and backsliding.

"Let us hold fast the confession of our hope without wavering, for he who promised is faithful. And let us consider how to stir up one another to love and good works, not neglecting to meet together, as is the habit of some, but encouraging one another, and all the more as you see the Day drawing near. For if we go on sinning deliberately after receiving the knowledge of the truth, there no longer remains a sacrifice for sins, but a fearful expectation of judgment, and a fury of fire that will consume the adversaries. Anyone who has set aside the law of Moses dies without mercy on

the evidence of two or three witnesses. How much worse punishment, do you think, will be deserved by the one who has trampled underfoot the Son of God, and has profaned the blood of the covenant by which he was sanctified, and has outraged the Spirit of grace? For we know him who said, 'Vengeance is mine; I will repay.' And again, 'The Lord will judge his people.' It is a fearful thing to fall into the hands of the living God. But recall the former days when, after you were enlightened, you endured a hard struggle with sufferings, sometimes being publicly exposed to reproach and affliction, and sometimes being partners with those so treated. For you had compassion on those in prison, and you joyfully accepted the plundering of your property, since you knew that you yourselves had a better possession and an abiding one. Therefore do not throw away your confidence, which has a great reward. For you have need of endurance, so that when you have done the will of God you may receive what is promised. For, 'Yet a little while, and the coming one will come and will not delay; but my righteous one shall live by faith, and if he shrinks back, my soul has no pleasure in him.' But we are not of those who shrink back and are destroyed, but of those who have faith and preserve their souls." (Hebrews 10:23-39)

The Bible is talking to Christians here, and if there was no danger at all of some of them turning away from God because of the persecution they are experiencing at this time, absolutely none of this passage would make any sense. They are saved. They have acquired a knowledge of the truth. They have been consecrated by the covenant blood. They have been spiritually enlightened. They had knowledge and consciousness that they had a better and lasting possession in heaven that allowed them to sacrifice their lives here. They had a fearless confidence. If they were not saved, then they were some supernatural sinners! But God's Word had to encourage and warn them to keep holding on and not let their troubles cause them to draw back to eternal misery and be utterly destroyed. Whoever they were, none of this makes sense if eternal damnation were not a possibility for them.

Eternal security proponents usually argue that the above Hebrews Scriptures are talking only about certain people under certain conditions, perhaps hypothetical but not real conditions, and therefore these Scriptures do not really prove anything at all. But why would the writer go through all of those scenarios hypothetically if they were impossible to ever occur. And whoever these Scriptures are referring to, under whatever set of conditions, this fact remains: Somebody here had experienced all of the major blessings of salvation through belief in Christ, spiritual enlightenment and a knowledge of the truth, cleansing by His blood of covenant, Holy Spirit infilling, assurance of heaven, fearless confidence, etc. What more could we expect them to have? But they lost it, or gave it up. Why and how it was lost does not matter here. The fact that it was lost reveals the fact that it is possible to lose it.

Several other pertinent Scriptures
Matthew 24:9-13
"They will deliver you up to tribulation and put you to death, and you will be hated by all nations for my name's sake. And then many will fall away and betray one another and hate one another. And many false prophets will arise and lead many astray. And because lawlessness will be increased, the love of many will grow cold. But the one who endures to the end will be saved."
In these verses Jesus teaches that in the last days there will be those who turn away from Him and quit following Him. His warning is clear: you must remain faithful to the end!

Luke 8:11-15
"The seed is the word of God. The ones along the path are those who have heard; then the devil comes and takes away the word from their hearts, so that they may not believe and be saved. And the ones on the rock are those who, when they hear the word, receive it with joy. But these have no root; they believe for a while, and in time of testing fall away. And as for what fell among the thorns, they are those who hear, but as they go on their way they are choked by the cares and riches and pleasures of life, and their fruit does not mature. As for that in the good soil, they are those who, hearing the word, hold it fast in an honest and good heart, and bear fruit with patience."

In this parable four different types of people are mentioned. The first group never become Christians but the last three are believers.

The last two remain steadfast in their faith but the second one has a serious problem. There is no doubt that at first the second group accepts Christ but they "fall away." It clearly says that they are believers. These are not people who "were never really Christians" as some churches teach. To say that someone who does not remain in the faith was never really saved in the first place is to create "eternal insecurity!" How do you know that you will persevere? Maybe you're not really a Christian after all! Fortunately the Lord doesn't leave us hanging. He says in *1 John 5:13 "I write this to you who believe in the name of the Son of God, that you may know that you have eternal life."* You notice He doesn't say, "hope" you have eternal life, or "got a good chance" at having eternal life.

Luke 12:45-46
"But if that servant says to himself, 'My master is delayed in coming,' and begins to beat the male and female servants, and to eat and drink and get drunk, the master of that servant will come on a day when he does not expect him and at an hour he does not know, and will cut him in pieces and put him with the unfaithful."

John 15:2-6
"Every branch in me that does not bear fruit he takes away, and every branch that does bear fruit he prunes, that it may bear more fruit. Already you are clean because of the word that I have spoken to you. Abide in me, and I in you. As the branch cannot bear fruit by itself, unless it abides in the vine, neither can you, unless you abide in me. I am the vine; you are the branches. Whoever abides in me and I in him, he it is that bears much fruit, for apart from me you can do nothing. If anyone does not abide in me he is thrown away like a branch and withers; and the branches are gathered, thrown into the fire, and burned."

Note that at one time the life of the Vine actually flowed in and through him, but now being separated from the Vine because of a refusal to bear Christian fruit, he loses that life.

Romans 11:17-23
"But if some of the branches were broken off, and you, although a wild olive shoot, were grafted in among the others and now share

in the nourishing root of the olive tree, do not be arrogant toward the branches. If you are, remember it is not you who support the root, but the root that supports you. Then you will say, 'Branches were broken off so that I might be grafted in.' That is true. They were broken off because of their unbelief, but you stand fast through faith. So do not become proud, but fear. For if God did not spare the natural branches, neither will he spare you. Note then the kindness and the severity of God: severity toward those who have fallen, but God's kindness to you, provided you continue in his kindness. Otherwise you too will be cut off. And even they, if they do not continue in their unbelief, will be grafted in, for God has the power to graft them in again."

Ever since the time of Abraham the Jews have been God's people. Their relationship with Him has been tumultuous at best but the Gospel was still made available to them first. If they believed in Jesus then they continued in God's grace. But, if they rejected him then they were removed but still given the option of coming back to Christ if they believed. The same is true for Christians. We are saved because we believe. If we reject Christ after salvation then we are cut off as well.

1 Corinthians 9:27
"I discipline my body and keep it under control, lest after preaching to others I myself should be disqualified."

If the Apostle Paul did not continue to keep his body in obedience, he would have been thrown away. That means salvation is not automatically kept. But we have to meet the conditions to keep it.

1 Corinthians 10:12
"Let any one who thinks that he stands take heed lest he fall."

This caution shows that the position is not guaranteed.

1 Corinthians 15:1-2
"Now I would remind you, brothers, of the gospel I preached to you, which you received, in which you stand, and by which you are being saved, if you hold fast to the word I preached to you—unless you believed in vain."

"If you hold fast" is conditional. If they do not keep faithful to the preaching, they lose the position of salvation.

Galatians 5:4
"You are severed from Christ, you who would be justified by the law; you have fallen away from grace."

They were in grace and hence they were saved. Now they fell from grace. That is, salvation is lost.

Colossians 1:21-23
"And you, who once were alienated and hostile in mind, doing evil deeds, he has now reconciled in his body of flesh by his death, in order to present you holy and blameless and above reproach before him, if indeed you continue in the faith, stable and steadfast, not shifting from the hope of the gospel that you heard..."

This letter is written to the *"The saints and faithful brothers in Christ at Colossae." (Colossians 1:2)* If, as Calvinists say, the truly saved cannot fall away, this whole admonition is unnecessary.

So perhaps this was written to those in the church who are not truly saved. This is a popular argument of some individuals. People who appear to lose their salvation were never saved in the first place. However, the instructions here make no sense for them, because why would Paul tell them to "continue in the faith" that does not lead to salvation anyway? Furthermore, why would he tell them not to be shifting away from some position they have never attained? A person cannot "move away from a place he was never in. One cannot lose something he never had.

So it is obvious that he was not talking to or about unsaved people, thus meaning that his instructions were definitely directed to those truly saved. He is warning the saved; he makes it conditional that the saved will be saved in the end if they continue and are not moved away. The only way this can make any sense at all is if it applies to the saved! Thus, we are forced to admit the possibility that the saved, if they disobey Paul's admonition and fail to continue, or allow themselves to be moved away, will not be saved after all. In other words, the saved can fall away and be lost.

1 Timothy 4:1-2
"Now the Spirit expressly says that in later times some will depart from the faith by devoting themselves to deceitful spirits and teachings of demons, through the insincerity of liars whose consciences are seared..."

The Holy Spirit says clearly that some saved persons will depart from the faith and will be lost. To deny that is to question what the Holy Spirit is saying, which is very dangerous.

Hebrews 3:12-14
"Take care, brothers, lest there be in any of you an evil, unbelieving heart, leading you to fall away from the living God. But exhort one another every day, as long as it is called 'today,' that none of you may be hardened by the deceitfulness of sin. For we have come to share in Christ, if indeed we hold our original confidence firm to the end."

"If" is a small word but it has a huge impact on this verse. Sharing in all that belongs to Christ is contingent upon remaining faithful to Him. The warning in this passage is to be very careful against being deceived and turning away from the faith. This warning is clearly to people who are already Christians. This concern would have no meaning at all if it were not possible for someone to loose their relationship with Christ. There is nothing in Scripture that supports the idea that you can be "out of fellowship" with the Lord here on earth and be "in fellowship" once you die.

James 5:19-20
"My brothers, if anyone among you wanders from the truth and someone brings him back, let him know that whoever brings back a sinner from his wandering will save his soul from death and will cover a multitude of sins."

If a saved person errs from the truth, it apparently makes him a sinner who needs to be saved again. Saving him from the error is saving his soul. That is, any time you go into error or go back into sin, you no longer have the salvation you once had.

2 Peter 2:20-21
"For if, after they have escaped the defilements of the world through the knowledge of our Lord and Savior Jesus Christ, they

are again entangled in them and overcome, the last state has become worse for them than the first. For it would have been better for them never to have known the way of righteousness than after knowing it to turn back from the holy commandment delivered to them."

If one eventually made it to heaven while being "out of fellowship" on earth then that would certainly be better than not believing in the first place! The warning in this Scripture clearly teaches that to know the Lord and then fall away puts a person in a very dangerous position. They no longer have salvation. As a matter of fact, after knowing the Lord their rejection of the knowledge of God hardens their hearts and makes it less likely that they will again come back to where they need to be spiritually.

Revelation 2:5
"Remember therefore from where you have fallen; repent, and do the works you did at first. If not, I will come to you and remove your lampstand from its place, unless you repent."

They had fallen from salvation. Jesus Christ requires them to repent and get back.

Revelation 3:15-16
"I know your works: you are neither cold nor hot. Would that you were either cold or hot! So, because you are lukewarm, and neither hot nor cold, I will spit you out of my mouth."

This church at first was living very close to God. Now God will spit them out unless they become hot for God. Getting "spit out" of God's mouth doesn't sound very eternally secure!

Revelation 3:5
"The one who conquers will be clothed thus in white garments, and I will never blot his name out of the book of life. I will confess his name before my Father and before his angels."

Revelation 20:14-15
"Then Death and Hades were thrown into the lake of fire. This is the second death, the lake of fire. And if anyone's name was not found written in the book of life, he was thrown into the lake of fire."

If you were "once saved, always saved" why would the Lord threaten to erase a person's name out of the book of life if that were impossible? These people at first are saved, meaning that God has written their names in the book of life. But, if they reject His word, God Himself will take their names out of the book of life, meaning that they are not saved any more. Then, whoever is not found in the book of life will be thrown into the lake of fire. So ultimately, these who were once saved are now thrown into the lake of fire.

There are many verses if studied carefully teach conditional salvation. Some are listed below for your personal consideration.

Matthew 13   *Romans 6:11-23*
Matthew 18:21-35   *Romans 8:12-14; 17*
Matthew 25:1-13   *Galatians 6:7-9*
John 6:66-71   *Philippians 2:12-16*
John 8:31-32; 51   *Hebrews 3:6-19*
Acts 14:21-22

Eternal Security Tends to Prevent Practical Holiness

It should also be noted that the doctrine of practical holiness, i.e., daily living with victory over sin, is generally incompatible with eternal security, the teaching that once a person is saved, the person is saved forever, no matter what they do or how rebelliously they live thereafter. This does not mean that no one who believes in eternal security can live holy. We simply mean that the doctrine of eternal security removes the "teeth" out of the requirement to live holy, thus permitting a generally lower standard of Christian behavior throughout the Body of Christ.

Once we remove the need to live holy and be submissive to God as one of the requirements to enter heaven, most real motivation to live a holy life is lost. Holiness becomes optional. If a person's life does not have to be clean and holy to remain in fellowship with God or to enter heaven in the end, then we begin to wonder why did Jesus Christ come and die and what is the point of a great portion of the Bible that continually exhorts us to holiness and daily victory over sin?

The writer of Hebrews said, *"Strive for peace with everyone, and for the holiness without which no one will see the Lord..." (Hebrews 12:14)*. Obviously, he is not talking about positional holiness or right standing with God (hosiotes in *Luke 1:75* and *Ephesians 4:24*), which a believer cannot do for himself. Instead he is referring to practical, character - and behavior based holiness ("hagiasmos and "hagiosune in *Romans 6:19* and *22*; *2 Corinthians 7:1; 1 Timothy 2:15*; and *1 Thessalonians 3:13 and 4:7*), which every believer is perfectly capable of and required to maintain. There should be no expectation of seeing the Lord, i.e., of enjoying His divine presence in heaven, without practicing holy living.

Resolving the Controversy

While we are on this subject, it would be good to make an attempt to resolve the conflict between practical holiness and the doctrine of eternal security. First of all, it should be noted that if a person believes in eternal security but still lives holy, then it doesn't matter whether their belief in "once saved always saved " is right or wrong. A belief in eternal security is only detrimental when a person dishonestly uses it as an excuse to continue living sinfully. Unfortunately, this is often done. Multitudes of "Christians" continue living a sinful lifestyle by assuming that once they made a decision for Christ, then it doesn't matter how awful their behavior might be; they are still saved.

But the Bible clearly teaches that sin can break fellowship with God *(2 Corinthians 6:14)*. However, when a Christian commits a sinful deed, this does not necessarily or immediately break fellowship with God. He gives the Christian committing the sin a space or time to repent *(Revelation 2:21)*. The Holy Spirit convicts the sinning Christian to repent, make restitution, clean up the situation, apologize to those offended, etc. Forgiveness is thus obtained, and the Christian's fellowship with God remains unbroken.

See also *1 John 1:5-2:6* regarding this process of sinning and restoration:
"This is the message we have heard from him and proclaim to you, that God is light, and in him is no darkness at all. If we say we have fellowship with him while we walk in darkness, we lie and do not

practice the truth. But if we walk in the light, as he is in the light, we have fellowship with one another, and the blood of Jesus his Son cleanses us from all sin. If we say we have no sin, we deceive ourselves, and the truth is not in us. If we confess our sins, he is faithful and just to forgive us our sins and to cleanse us from all unrighteousness. If we say we have not sinned, we make him a liar, and his word is not in us. My little children, I am writing these things to you so that you may not sin. But if anyone does sin, we have an advocate with the Father, Jesus Christ the righteous. He is the propitiation for our sins, and not for ours only but also for the sins of the whole world. And by this we know that we have come to know him, if we keep his commandments. Whoever says 'I know him' but does not keep his commandments is a liar, and the truth is not in him, but whoever keeps his word, in him truly the love of God is perfected. By this we may know that we are in him: whoever says he abides in him ought to walk in the same way in which he walked."

If the Christian refuses to respond to the convictions of the Holy Spirit and refuses to repent for the wrong deed done, the Holy Spirit will continue to prod and persuade him or her to repent, to straighten up the situation, and to remove the stain of guilt from his record and his heart and mind. How do we know this? Because verse 9 is, once again, a tautology: *"If we confess our sins, he is faithful and just to forgive us our sins and to cleanse us from all unrighteousness."* It logically follows that if we do not confess, then He does not forgive or cleanse. Why would God forgive the sins of someone who does not have a heart and attitude of repentance, regret, humility, and confession? Such would be a complete violation of the whole biblical concept of confession and repentance!

So if the sinning Christian never repents or confesses, the Holy Spirit eventually ceases to deal with him about the matter, eventually breaking fellowship with God. "Whoever says 'I know him' but does not keep his commandments is a liar, and the truth is not in him." People who are not in fellowship with God do not go to heaven, not even to receive a lower degree of rewards. People out of fellowship with God go to hell. Indeed, that is the only way to get there: Simply be out of fellowship with God! People out of fellowship with God remain in spiritual death.

The traditional, non-Calvinistic Christian doctrine is similar to eternal security in that it does not teach that every little sin and misdeed results in an immediate loss of fellowship with God. We don't just "lose our salvation" for every little misdeed or without our knowledge. However, it does differ from eternal security by teaching that every willful and wrong deed you are aware of must be confessed and repented of to maintain fellowship with God. And it differs by teaching that a person who willfully rebels and refuses to repent for his known sins eventually falls out of fellowship with God and cannot enter heaven (Only God knows the exact time when that happens.).

Some well-known eternal security teachers actually teach that once saved, a person can sin, deliberately turn his back completely on God, and even become an unbeliever, but still make it into heaven because of that one point in time in which that person made a decision for Christ! They teach that even if a believer, for all practical purposes becomes an unbeliever, his salvation is not in jeopardy. Why not? Because these false teachers say, "A man or woman who has been rescued once from a state of unforgiveness need not worry. For once 100% of a man's or woman's sins have been forgiven, the potential for being unforgiven has been done away with. The risk factor is zero. There are no more fires from which the believer needs to be saved. Of course, this reasoning contradicts the above clear teachings of Scripture. But **to give people a false hope of salvation when they are not really Christians is a terrible danger!** People who are falsely taught that they are secure when the Bible says they are not is one of the greatest sins possible! Those who teach the eternal security doctrine run the risk of excusing sin, justifying selfishness, redefining what is morally right and wrong in society, permitting sin and selfishness in the church, and deceiving people into thinking that they, or others they know, who were once Christians can eventually make it to heaven no matter how they live.

"I charge you in the presence of God and of Christ Jesus, who is to judge the living and the dead, and by his appearing and his

kingdom: preach the word; be ready in season and out of season; reprove, rebuke, and exhort, with complete patience and teaching. For the time is coming when people will not endure sound teaching, but having itching ears they will accumulate for themselves teachers to suit their own passions, and will turn away from listening to the truth and wander off into myths." (2 Timothy 4:1-4)

Please... Don't be the preacher (or Christian) warned about in this Scripture. Instead be bold enough to follow the truth wherever Scripture may lead.

Appendix 2

Spiritual Gifts

What are spiritual gifts?
Throughout history there has been a lot of discussion about spiritual gifts. At times the gifts were totally ignored and then at other times certain gifts were overly emphasized almost to the total exclusion of all of the other gifts.

According to the Bible spiritual gifts are special abilities given by God to strengthen the Body of Christ (born again believers).

Why do you need to know about spiritual gifts?
1. They will benefit you in your life.
2. They will benefit the Church Body.
3. They will help you know God's will for your life.

What is the difference between spiritual gifts and the Fruit of the Spirit (Galatians 5:22-23)?

Spiritual Gifts	Fruit of the Spirit
Christian Service	Ethical Character
Easier to imitate	Difficult to imitate
Outward actions	Inward attitudes
Individually specific	For all Spirit filled believers

What happens if you decide not to discover, develop and use your spiritual gift?
1. The "Body of Christ" will be weakened
2. God's Glory in your life will be diminished
What is the purpose of spiritual gifts?
1. Edification of the Church
2. Extension of the Church

Note: No gift has a primary purpose for the individual. It is always primarily for the betterment of the Body of Christ.

How are spiritual gifts most effective?
When used in an attitude of love and service to the Body of Christ (1 Corinthians 13)

Can a person have more than one spiritual gift?

A person can have as many Spiritual Gifts as God chooses to give him or her. Some even have "spiritual" gifts not mentioned in the Bible but are obvious to others, such as the gift of music. However, usually one gift is the most dominant. In practical application we call that gift your "Motivational Gift." Understanding your motivational gift can help you focus on becoming more effective in the development of your gift. Recognizing other's gifts can help in understanding the differences between Christians in their approaches to life and ministry.

Important things to remember:

1. Even though we have one major motivational gift, we are to practice the positive characteristics of all of the gifts.
2. All gifts are important and need to be understood and exercised in the Body of Christ.
3. Spiritual gifts are given by God and not chosen by individuals.
4. An individual's value or worth is not raised or lowered by what spiritual gift they have.
5. Spiritual gifts are never to be a source of ungodly pride.

"For by the grace given to me I say to everyone among you not to think of himself more highly than he ought to think, but to think with sober judgment, each according to the measure of faith that God has assigned. For as in one body we have many members, and the members do not all have the same function, so we, though many, are one body in Christ, and individually members one of another." (Romans 12:3-5)

Spiritual Gifts in *Romans 12*

The Bible mentions several different kinds of spiritual gifts but in this study we will focus on the gifts mentioned in the book of Romans. The Apostle Paul lists 7 gifts in Romans Chapter 12. Even though different translations describe them differently they essentially are: Prophecy, Serving, Teaching, Exhortation, Giving, Leadership and Mercy.

"Having gifts that differ according to the grace given to us, let us use them: if prophecy, in proportion to our faith; if service, in our serving; the one who teaches, in his teaching; the one who exhorts,

in his exhortation; the one who contributes, in generosity; the one who leads, with zeal; the one who does acts of mercy, with cheerfulness." (Romans 12:6-8)

Each of these gifts has certain characteristics that can be recognized in the life of the person with that particular gift. There are also possible misuses of each gift. After listing the spiritual gifts in Romans 12 the Bible gives us specific instruction on how we should live our lives.

"Let love be genuine. Abhor what is evil; hold fast to what is good. Love one another with brotherly affection. Outdo one another in showing honor. Do not be slothful in zeal, be fervent in spirit, serve the Lord. Rejoice in hope, be patient in tribulation, be constant in prayer. Contribute to the needs of the saints and seek to show hospitality. Bless those who persecute you; bless and do not curse them. Rejoice with those who rejoice, weep with those who weep. Live in harmony with one another. Do not be haughty, but associate with the lowly. Never be wise in your own sight. Repay no one evil for evil, but give thought to do what is honorable in the sight of all. If possible, so far as it depends on you, live peaceably with all. Beloved, never avenge yourselves, but leave it to the wrath of God, for it is written, 'Vengeance is mine, I will repay, says the Lord.' To the contrary, 'if your enemy is hungry, feed him; if he is thirsty, give him something to drink; for by so doing you will heap burning coals on his head.' Do not be overcome by evil, but overcome evil with good." (Romans 12:9-21)

Spiritual Gifts Questionnaire
(Only mark the top 15 that best describe you)

1. _____You want to make sure that statements are true and accurate.
2. _____You can visualize the final result of a major undertaking.
3. _____You see actions as either right or wrong.
4. _____You sense when people have hurt feelings.
5. _____You motivate people to become what you see they could be.

6. _____You notice the practical needs of others and enjoy meeting them.
7. _____You are very frugal with money for yourself and your family.
8. _____You desire to gain as much knowledge as you can.
9. _____You enjoy coordinating the efforts of many to reach a common goal.
10. _____You react strongly to people who are not what they appear to be.
11. _____You react to those who are insensitive to other's feelings.
12. _____You like to give counsel in logical steps of action.
13. _____You enjoy serving to free others for more important things.
14. _____You enjoy investing money in the ministries of other people.
15. _____You react to people who make unfounded statements.
16. _____You can break down a large task into achievable goals.
17. _____You can usually detect when something is not what it appears to be.
18. _____You are able to discern genuine love.
19. _____You can usually discern a person's level of spiritual maturity.
20. _____You are willing to neglect your own work to help others.
21. _____You have an ability to make money by wise investments.
22. _____You check the credentials of one who wants to teach you.
23. _____You are able to delegate assignments to others.
24. _____You can quickly discern a person's character.
25. _____You desire deep friendships in which there is mutual commitment.
26. _____You enjoy working out projects to help people grow spiritually.
27. _____You sometimes go beyond your physical strength in serving others.
28. _____You desire to keep your giving a secret.

29. _____You use your mind to check out an argument.
30. _____You see people as resources that can be used to get a job done.
31. _____You feel a responsibility to correct those who do wrong.
32. _____You seem to attract people who tell you their problems.
33. _____You sometimes raise expectations of results prematurely
34. _____You can remember the likes and dislikes of others.
35. _____You react negatively to pressure appeals for money.
36. _____You enjoy spending hours doing research on a subject.
37. _____You are willing to endure reaction in order to accomplish a task
38. _____You separate yourself from those who refuse to repent of evil.
39. _____You find it difficult to be firm or decisive with people.
40. _____You dislike teaching that does not give practical direction.
41. _____You can usually detect ways to serve before anyone else can.
42. _____You like to encourage others to give with your gifts.
43. _____You like to tell others as many facts as you can on a topic.
44. _____You require loyalty in those who are under your supervision.
45. _____You explain what is wrong with an item before you sell it.
46. _____You tend to take up offenses for those whom you love
47. _____You like to see the facial responses of those whom you counsel.
48. _____You will even use your own funds to get a job done quickly.
49. _____You want the ministries you support to be as effective as possible.
50. _____You pay attention to words and phrases.
51. _____You remove yourself from petty details to focus on the final goal.

52. _____You let people know how you feel about important issues.
53. _____You need quality time to explain how you feel.
54. _____You often take "family time" to counsel others.
55. _____You do not mind doing jobs by yourself.
56. _____You enjoy giving to need which others tend to overlook.
57. _____You tend to be silent on matters until you check it out.
58. _____You can encourage your workers and inspire them to action.
59. _____You enjoy people who are completely honest with you.
60. _____You want to remove those who cause hurts to others.
61. _____You enjoy giving examples from the lives of others.
62. _____You do not want public praise, but you do need to feel appreciated.
63. _____You sometimes fear that your gifts will corrupt those who get them.
64. _____You like to study material in a systematic sequence.
65. _____You move on to a new challenge once a job is finished.
66. _____You are quick to judge yourself when you fail.
67. _____You often wonder why God allows people to suffer.
68. _____You soon give up on those who do not follow your counsel.
69. _____You find it difficult to say "no" to those who ask for help.
70. _____You desire to give gifts of high quality.
71. _____You present truth in a logical, systematic way.
72. _____You are highly motivated to organize that for which you are responsible.
73. _____You are willing to do right even if it means suffering alone for it.
74. _____You sense the spiritual and emotional atmosphere of a group or individual.
75. _____You love to do personal counseling.
76. _____You may neglect your own family's needs by being too busy helping others.
77. _____You may upset family and friends with unpredictable patterns of giving.

STOP

Do not turn to the next page until you have selected the top 15 characteristics that best describe you.

Spiritual Gifts Answer Key

Teaching	Leadership/Organization	Prophecy	Mercy	Exhortation	Serving	Giving
1	2	3	4	5	6	7
8	9	10	11	12	13	14
15	16	17	18	19	20	21
22	23	24	25	26	27	28
29	30	31	32	33	34	35
36	37	38	39	40	41	42
43	44	45	46	47	48	49
50	51	52	53	54	55	56
57	58	59	60	61	62	63
64	65	66	67	68	69	70
71	72	73	74	75	76	77

My Spiritual Gift is: _____

Now that you've discovered your primary motivational spiritual gift, what do you do next?

1. Share with your pastor and others in the Church what you think your gift is.
2. Look for ways to practice your gift among the Body of Christ.
3. Pray that God will enhance and develop your gift for greater service.
4. If you can not decide between two different gifts do the following:
    1. Ask spiritually mature people who know you what they think your gift is.
    2. Take two questions you selected and choose between them.
    3. Practice what you think your gift is and see how fulfilled you are while doing it.
    3. Notice the characteristics and misuses of the specific gifts to help you decide which better describes you.

Characteristics and Possible Misuses of the Spiritual Gifts

Teaching	
Characteristic	**Misuse**
Need to validate information	Becoming proud of knowledge
Check out teachers	Despising lack of credentials
Rely on established resources	Depending on human reasoning
Present truth systematically	Criticizing practical applications
Gather many facts	Showing off research skills
Require thoroughness	Rejecting Scriptural presuppositions
Uneasy with subjective truth	Putting mind above the Holy Spirit
Persevere with accepted teachers	Taking teachings to extremes
Clarify misunderstandings	Arguing over minor points

Biblical example: Luke

When a teacher hears important statements, whether given privately or publicly, they will desire to verify them. Their motivation is to confirm that the statements are true and accurate. A possible temptation would be for the teacher to become proud of their knowledge. They may also appear to be prideful by giving far more information than is needed to prove a point.

A person with the gift of teaching will be very alert to false teachers. They will want to find out their background before listening to them. They will also assume that others want to know their qualifications; thus, they will tend to give these before speaking. Many teachers attempt to control misinformation by requiring approved courses of instruction or degrees from reputable institutions.

A teacher has a strong desire to go to primary sources to validate truth. They will also use accepted works of recognized authorities to further confirm statements that others make. Since the teacher is able to use scholarly resources, they may give the impression that they are the only source of truth and that their gift is more important than the other gifts.

Teachers tend to feel more comfortable when material is laid out in an orderly sequence. The teacher wants to know the events in the order in which they occurred. A teacher's motivation to verify all statements by the authority of Scripture may hinder them in making wider Scriptural application. As they focus on textual studies, they may miss the underlying principles that tie all Scripture together.

Those with the gift of teaching often have a greater delight in researching facts than they do in teaching them. When they do teach or speak they feel constrained to give as many facts as possible. Sometimes when they share a conclusion they feel obligated to explain how they arrived at it. The teacher may assume that others are as interested in the extensive research as they are when in reality they are not. A teacher enjoys giving details that are not noticed or mentioned by others. They are concerned that truth is presented in the correct order. Scripture is first then experience, never the other way around. A teacher tends to remain loyal to a mentor or a church as long as any truth remains and does what they can to promote the truth but they need to be careful to not take doctrine to extremes and argue over minor points.

Leadership/Organization	
Characteristic	Misuse
Able to visualize final results	Viewing people only as resources
Need loyalty in associates	Building loyalty with favoritism
Ability to delegate	Using delegation to avoid work
Withstand reaction to tasks	Being unresponsive to appeals
Make jobs look easy	Putting projects ahead of people
Very alert to details	Overlooking worker's serious faults
Complete tasks quickly	Failing to explain or praise
Able to be decisive	Forcing decisions on others
Completion involves cleanup	Losing interest in finished job

Biblical example: Nehemiah

When a major project is given to a leader, they are able to picture the completed task and what it will take to finish it. Leaders need to patiently explain all of the steps needed to accomplish something when dealing with others. They can become impatient and discouraged when others do not follow the specific plans. In order for a leader to visualize the completion of a task, they need to know who and what their resources are. A leader is very sensitive to loyalty. They depend upon it to accomplish their goals or the goals others have for them. Leaders may single out individuals whom they think are especially important to their goals and show them favoritism, which may cause disharmony with others.

A leader knows which tasks to delegate and which they must do themselves. They are able to sense which workers will need more assistance than others. Once a leader commits to a task they are willing to endure a lot of opposition to their leadership. They expect quick response and know that without the continuous pressures that they must exert that the final goal may not be achieved. Sometimes leaders will reject valid suggestions, which may cause some to drop out or reject their leadership. Leaders are able to devise an effective plan that makes complete sense to them but others may not see. Leaders are most effective when they have demonstrated in their own life that their leadership results in positive outcomes.

A leader has the ability to take seemingly impossible tasks and break them down into achievable goals. They may become frustrated with unorganized people and hinder interpersonal relationships. Leaders may also give instructions without explanation. This may cause fellow workers to feel like they are being used. Because the final goal is clearly visualized by the leader, they are able to quickly evaluate requests and situations and make firm decisions. They have a special ability to persuade others. They are decisive and very organized. For leaders the project is not complete until everything is finished. They will inspire and encourage others to complete a job by approval, praise, reproof and challenge. Leaders find fulfillment in completing projects. They can become frustrated with disorganization and clutter.

Prophecy	
Characteristic	Misuse
A need to express themselves	Exposing sin without restoration
Quick impressions of people	Jumping to conclusions
Alertness to dishonesty	Reacting harshly to sinners
Desire for justice	Being unforgiving
Open about their own faults	Condemning themselves
Wholehearted involvement	Being impetuous
Loyalty to truth	Cutting off people who fail
Willingness to suffer for right	Lacking tactfulness in rebuke
Persuasive in defining truth	Dwelling on the negative

Biblical example: Peter

Prophets need to express their thoughts and ideas verbally, especially when matters of right and wrong are involved. A prophet's primary concern about stopping the spread of evil tends to cause them to expose a sinner rather than restore them. They feel that the exposure of sin is the first step of restoration. Prophets tend to make quick judgments on what they see and hear. They also tend to express their view before others speak. Sometimes prophets will come to conclusions from only a few known facts, which can result in a wrong judgment. They may take the words and actions of others out of context to prove their point.

Prophets have an amazing ability to sense when someone or something is not what it appears to be. They react harshly to any form of deception or dishonesty. When a prophet sees sin, they tend to denounce it so strongly that it appears to others to be insensitive or intolerant. A prophet tends to expect immediate repentance regardless of whether their rebuke was given in love or was even fully accurate. Their motive is to promote repentance for sin. Prophets tend to cut off those who sin so that justice will be done and others will be warned. It is very difficult for a prophet to make a separation between sin and the sinner. As a result they tend to reject them both with equal vigor. Those who hear their harshness may interpret their denunciations as angry tirades.

Prophets are as open about their own failures as they want others to be about theirs. Prophets tend to be extremely self-critical and feel worthless when they fail. They are loyal to truth even if it means cutting off relationships. Whenever they see or hear something that is wrong, they feel responsible to speak out against it. They don't stop to think and ask: "Whose responsibility is this? Do I have all of the facts? Do I need to take action at this time or should I wait?"

Prophets are quick to suffer when it comes to standing for the truth or doing what is right. They tend to be painfully direct when correcting others, no matter who they are. This bluntness can cause embarrassment for everyone involved. Prophets have a special ability to be articulate in defining what is right and what is wrong. They tend to see everything as either right or wrong with no middle ground and they often feel compelled to persuade others to agree with them

Mercy	
Characteristic	**Misuse**
Deeply loyal to friends	Taking up offenses
Need for deep friendships	Becoming possessive
Empathize with hurting people	Tolerating evil
Decisions based on benefits	Failing to be firm
Deeply sensitive to loved ones	Leaning on emotions vs. reason
Attract people in distress	Defrauding opposite sex
Desire to remove hurts	Reacting to God's purposes
Measure acceptance by closeness	Failing to show deference
Attracted to Prophets	Cutting off insensitive people

Biblical example: John

A person with the gift of mercy will demonstrate loyalty to a friend even by reacting harshly toward those who attack them. The tendency of one with the gift of mercy is to take up an offense for someone who is being hurt by another person. The very nature of a person with the gift of mercy requires close friendships. These friendships, however, must have mutual commitment, which is often reaffirmed. This need for a close friendship can cause them to monopolize the time and attention of others. As they experience disappointments in one friendship, the person with mercy tends to place greater demands on a new friendship.

The gift of mercy enables the one having it to sense which individuals are hurting and to share the pain with them. Along with the pain, a mercy senses the full scope of emotions. If those with the gift of mercy do not have spiritual discernment as to why people suffer, they may give sympathy and encouragement to those who are suffering as a direct result of violating God's moral laws. They find it hard to be firm because they do not want to offend other people. They need to see that greater hurt and offenses may occur if they fail to be decisive. When a person with the gift of mercy is given a position of leadership, they will tend to avoid disciplinary actions that are needed. As a result, the person who should have been disciplined is not brought to repentance and prophets may react to the mercy's leadership with other mercies reacting to the prophets!

A mercy has the ability to sense genuine love. They have a greater vulnerability to deeper and more frequent hurts from those who fail to demonstrate sincere love. Because those with the gift of mercy have such sensitive feelings, they tend to base their decisions on emotions rather than on principles. Their subjective reasoning can easily cause them to reject Biblical doctrines that seem harsh to them.

One with the gift of mercy has a deep understanding of people who are going through mental or emotional distress. This sensitivity causes those with hurts to be drawn to them and to confide in them. Mercy's have a desire for physical closeness in order to be reassured of acceptance.

Exhortation	
Characteristic	**Misuse**
Committed to spiritual growth	Keeping others waiting for them
Able to see root problems	Looking to themselves for solutions
See steps of action	Being proud of visible results
Raise hope for solutions	Starting projects prematurely
Turn problems into benefits	Treating people as projects
Desire to be "transparent"	Sharing private illustrations
Gain insight through experience	Presenting truth out of balance
Urgency to act on clear steps	Setting unrealistic goals
Desire to share face to face	Giving up on uncooperative people

Biblical example: Paul

The motivation of an exhorter is to see spiritual growth take place in practical living, and they are willing to become personally involved to see it achieved. An exhorter's willingness to give people whatever time is necessary to help them grow spiritually often cuts into other time commitments. They assume that others will understand why they are not spending time with them or they are late for appointments.

An exhorter can discern the spiritual maturity of another person. Based on this, the exhorter is motivated to search out hindrances in the lives of those who are not growing spiritually and to give further encouragement to those who are. They will often use examples from the lives of others to help Christians see the potential of daily victory. Sometimes an exhorter will not listen carefully and will categorize problems causing them to arrive at conclusions before getting all of the facts. They are especially interested in spiritual growth and can visualize spiritual achievement for another Christian and then help them work out practical steps of action to achieve it. These steps are designed to remove hindrances and develop personal disciplines through which the Holy Spirit can work. When an exhorter gives steps of action, they assume that they will be carried out. If people don't respond quickly and consistently to the steps of action the Exhorter may loose hope. As spiritual growth becomes visible, an exhorter needs to be careful about taking personal credit for it.

Exhorters tend to jump into new projects without finishing existing ones. They use projects to motivate others, and then when others are involved, the exhorter finds a better project. After several projects, those who are working on them may become frustrated. The exhorter, however, sees the projects as simply a means to accomplishing a bigger perspective. Mature exhorters have learned by experience that God gives special grace during trials. They know that true growth will not take place where there is guilt. As a result they tend to be very open about their life and expect others to be that way as well. Exhorters tend to avoid heavy doctrinal teaching that does not have immediate practical application. The result of this emphasis can be an imbalance of teaching that may eventually show up as doctrinal error. The exhorter can greatly benefit from the influence of a teacher.

Serving	
Characteristic	Misuse
See & meet practical needs	Giving unrequested help
Free others to achieve	Letting things be too important
Disregard for weariness	Working beyond physical limits
Difficulty in saying "no"	Neglecting God-given priorities
Alert to likes and dislikes	Reacting to overlooked needs
Need approval	Resenting lack of appreciation
Like short-range projects	Working people around their schedule
Put extra touches to jobs	Being frustrated with time limits
Meet needs quickly	Interfering with God's discipline

Biblical example: Timothy

Important needs that would seem insignificant to others catch the eye and attention of the server. These needs are usually physical; however, the server knows that by meeting them they will bring encouragement and strength to those who receive their help. Sometimes the tasks that the server sees appear to be more important to the server than the one being served. It may even be that the one who has the need is not aware of it to the degree that the server is. In either case, a server who uses his initiative in meeting these needs may be judged as pushy or intrusive.

The joy of the server is not just initiating tasks, but knowing that through them they are bringing a peace of mind to another person that will allow that person to be more productive in the tasks that God has called them to do. In order to meet the needs of others, servers will often neglect their own home and personal responsibilities. Because the server sees the importance of the tasks that they have begun, they will freely use up personal assets of time, money and strength. Their focus is not on their self, but rather on the completion of the tasks, which they know will benefit the individual and bring joy. The sever may be so focused and driven to complete projects that they neglect their own health.

As the server effectively meets one need, others may ask for similar help, not realizing the inner motivation of the server. These requests, however, are difficult to turn down because they represent needs and the server feels obligated at having been asked. Servers are often placed in positions of responsibility because they are diligent workers. They are quick to volunteer but often have problems delegating tasks to others. They would rather do the work their self than ask others to do it.

Those with the gift of serving have an amazing ability to find out and remember the special interests of the people they serve. Servers may react to people around them who, in their judgment, walk right past obvious needs. They assume that others see what they see. If they tell someone about a need and that person doesn't follow through on their suggestion, the server may become resentful. Appreciation confirms to the server that their work is necessary and the Lord is blessing it. Servers need to be shown recognition and appreciation but prefer it to be private rather than public.

Giving

Characteristic	Misuse
Able to see resources	Hoarding resources for self
Invest self with gift	Using gift to control people
Desire to give high quality	Forcing higher living standards
Hope gift answers prayer	Feeling guilty about personal assets
Desire to give secretly	Rejecting pressure appeals
Concern that giving will corrupt	Giving too sparingly to family
Exercise personal thriftiness	Giving to projects vs. people
Use gifts to multiply giving	Causing people to look to him/her vs. God
Confirm amount with counsel	Waiting too long to give

Biblical example: Matthew

A giver has an ability to discern wise investments. Their motivation is to use assets of time, money, and possessions to advance the work of the Lord. If a person with the gift of giving has limited funds, they are still able to use their ability of recognizing available resources and draw upon them when needed. Because a giver is so careful with resources they may hoard items that should be given away. A giver needs continuous reassurance that their decisions are in

God's will whether he has little or much to give. A giver has a desire to make sure that their gifts are wisely invested and used. They will pay extra for good quality items but are careful to not over spend.

Givers are sensitive to the leading of the Lord and will give even when a need is not obvious. Their ultimate confirmation that this gift was according to God's will comes when they learn that it fulfilled an unknown need or answered a special prayer. Often givers give quietly and anonymously. A mature giver understands the destructiveness of the love of money. They are very aware that those who need their assistance may not have learned the disciplines that God taught them in acquiring assets. Therefore, they look for ways of giving which avoid dependency, slothfulness, or extravagance.

The personal assets that the giver has are often the result of consistent personal frugality while being content with basics. A giver will always be concerned in getting the best buy, not with how much they have left. They will spend extra effort in saving money and being resourceful with what they have. The motivation of a giver is to encourage others to give. They want others to experience the joy and spiritual growth that comes by sacrificial giving. As a result, the giver may provide matching funds or the last payment in order to encourage others to give.

A giver will not respond to emotional or pressure appeals. Instead they look for financial needs that others may overlook. If known, a giver's resourcefulness and assets may be a temptation for others. The giver needs to be in constant fellowship with the Lord to determine His will in whether to give or not to give to a specific request.

christiankarate.org

Made in the USA
Columbia, SC
18 November 2022

71553849R00078